The Mysterious World

The Mysterious World

By the Editors of Time-Life Books

TIME-LIFE BOOKS, ALEXANDRIA, VIRGINIA

CONTENTS

Maps of the Unknown

Nowhere have the mysteries of our planet been more exquisitely rendered than on old maps that in centuries past graced the halls of kings and popes and guided the travels of merchants and explorers. Although they bear scant resemblance to today's maps, these charts accurately depicted for their eras the known world as well as the wonders and terrors awaiting anyone who braved the unknown—including some locations that still retain a mysterious aura.

The thirteenth-century map at right, for example, puts Jerusalem at the very center of the world—appropriate even today, when Judaism, Christianity, and Islam each view the ancient city as a sacred focus, a place to connect to divine power. The map is a Christian creation, however, and presents the planet in terms of the medieval Christian mystery. It portrays the world as a flat disk with three continents—Asia at the top, Europe and Africa to the left and right, divided by the Mediterranean that runs upward from the lower right—all within the loving embrace of Jesus Christ, whose extremities mark the four cardinal directions. The landmarks from church history include the Garden of Eden and the burial places of saints such as Mark, Bartholomew, Philip, and Thomas.

Enfolding the world into Christ's body must have given solace to the map's creator, who drew a frightful race of humanoid monsters in Ethiopia, at far right. Moreover, the giants Gog and Magog, described in the Bible as forces of the Antichrist who will overrun the earth on Judgment Day, bide their time at upper left behind a mountain wall believed to have been erected by Alexander the Great. Good Christians neither doubted the barrier's existence nor questioned its purpose: It let them sleep at night.

On this world map from 1234, Christ's head is in the east (top), his feet in the west (bottom), and his hands at north and south, while the holy city of Jerusalem marks his navel.

Fabled Allies and Dread Enemies

Early explorers returning from faraway lands described a world stranger than most of their fellow Europeans had ever imagined. South America, said the travelers, was home to longhair deer, mountains brimming with silver, and native populations so wealthy they rolled their chieftains in gold. A beneficent white king was said to reign in the mountains, but bloodthirsty cannibals and cruel warrior women called Amazons held sway elsewhere. Anyone who dared invade their territories, it was rumored, would be made to suffer a horrible death. Travelers to the East told of similar empires, including that of a virtuous and powerful Christian king named Prester John. Hoping he would help Europe's crusades against Islam, expeditions searched for him in Asia, then in Africa *(right)*, but like the conquistadors who hacked through the rain forest looking for El Dorado, all came home empty-handed.

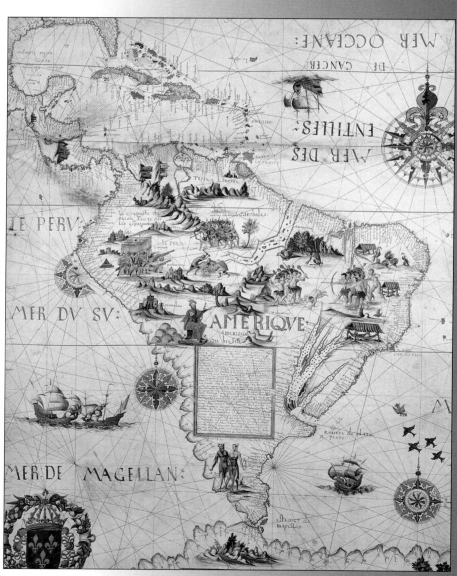

Above, a map of South America drawn in 1550 shows genuine placenames as well as cannibal armies, Amazon warriors, and the mysterious white king of the Andes Mountains (center).

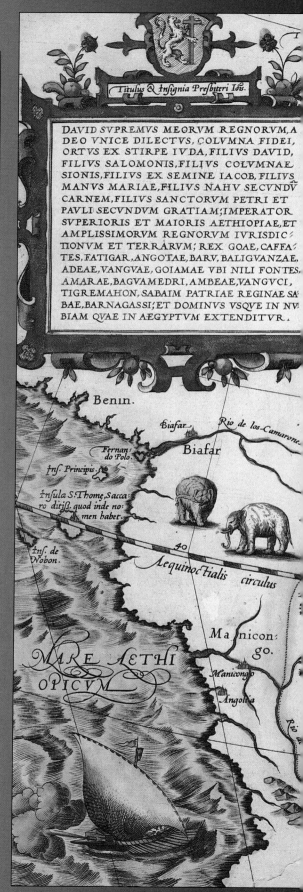

According to the 1573 chart at right, the empire of Prester John lay somewhere between the Mediterranean (top) and Africa's Mountains of the Moon (bottom), then thought to be the source of the river Nile.

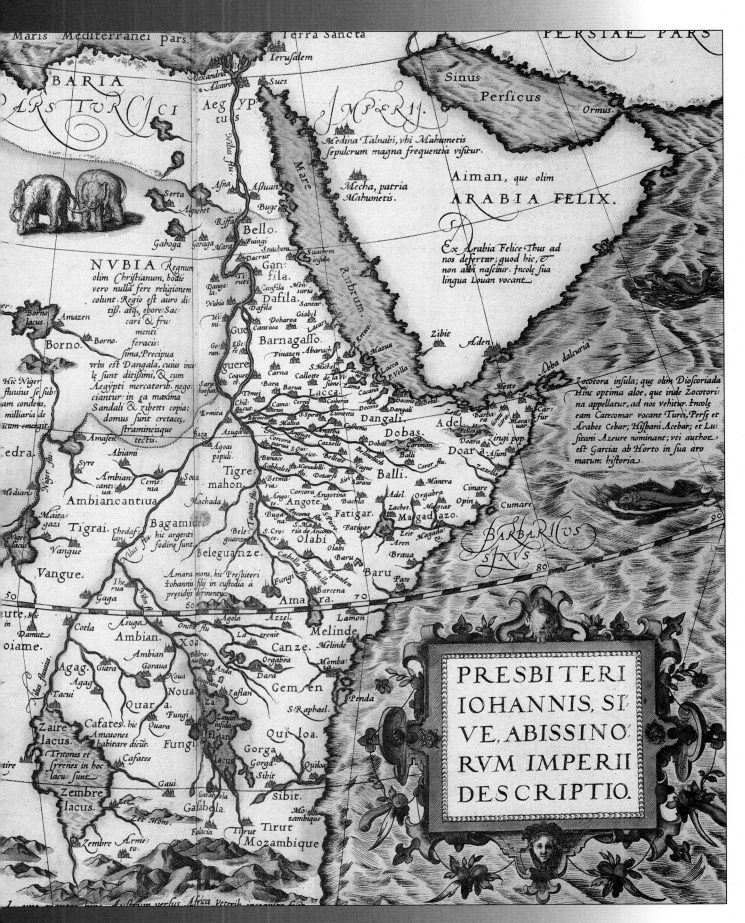

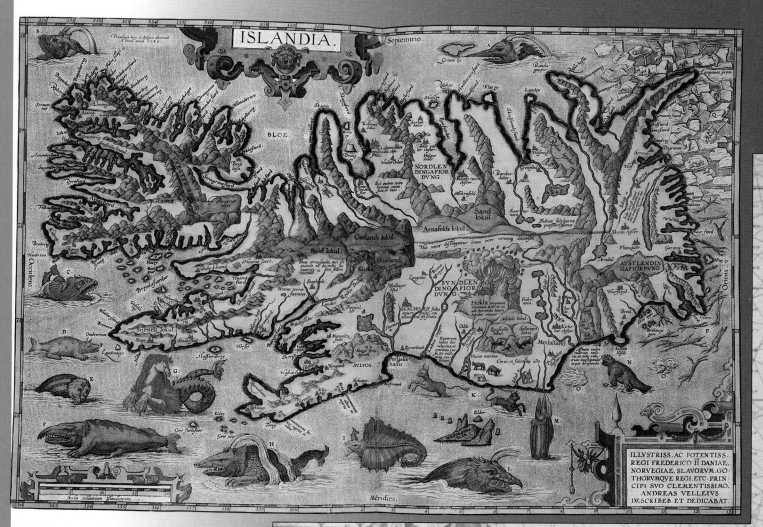

In this sixteenth-century Flemish engraving, exotic sea monsters patrol the waters to the south and west of Iceland, while bearlike beasts clamber over ice to the northeast.

Maned lions and a unicorn are counted among the fauna of the New World on this 1540 chart. North America's east coast is depicted upside down to the orientation usually employed nowadays; here Florida is at top right, Canada at bottom left.

Where the Unicorns Roam

On medieval maps, Europeans depicted remote regions of the planet as the
dwelling places of extraordinarily
freakish humanlike creatures—people
whose feet had eight toes and pointed
backward, men with talons for fingers
and the heads of dogs who barked for
speech, and many other monstrous
races. Of course, when the intrepid
explorers of the fifteenth and sixteenth
centuries finally gazed into the distant
corners of the world, they found no
such monsters. But they did come
across a multitude of animals, birds,
and sea creatures that until then had
escaped registry in European bestiar-
ies. At a loss to name the animals, the
discoverers wrote colorful descriptions
of them. Their accounts, repeated
frequently and sometimes exaggerated,
formed the basis for a new generation
of maps, such as these. Here, the animals are used not only to convey a
sense of the wonder of the mysterious
New World, but also to fill in those
territories yet to be explored—which
the mapmakers otherwise would have
had to leave blank.

Charting the Heavens

Astrologers were the early cartographers of the skies. Looking up at the stars, they not only saw in the constellations a host of gods, heroes, and other extraordinary beings accepted as totally real, but they also believed they sensed powerful emanations of an invisible life force that permeated the world and held together the four lower elements of earth, air, fire, and water. The astrologers' work was put to more practical use, too, because it provided a guide for travelers who navigated by the stars as well as for people steering their lives by the powers of the heavenly bodies.

Although animated by characters considered mythical by then, this 1590 chart of the Northern skies was useful to both astrologers and sailors.

13

The Southern Hemisphere, too, abounds with mythical figures, including hunter Orion and the Argo (center), the ship Jason sailed to seek the golden fleece.

The Earth on a Platter

Some of the world's most sought-after lands, though included on many maps, have yet to be discovered. Explorers using the old charts are not easily deterred, however, because the lands they seek are storied lost continents, perhaps holding answers to some of history's most vexing puzzles.

One mystery concerns the lemur: What trick of evolution permitted this tree-dwelling species to be found only in two widely separated places, India and Madagascar? Some maintain that these areas were once connected by a land that sank, never to be seen again. For reasons unclear, many occultists now think this continent—known as Lemuria or Mu—lies under the Pacific *(far right, top)* rather than under the Indian Ocean. They believe it accounts not only for the distribution of the lemur, but also for the birth of humankind.

Similarly, some theorists say only the existence of fabled Atlantis *(far right, bottom)* can explain the baffling origin of ancient American civilizations, once highly advanced but now lost. Meanwhile, those who endorse the accuracy of the reasonable-looking map at near right are not seeking any lost continents. They simply contend the world is flat.

Ice and darkness ring the world as pictured here by the Flat Earth Society. Members believe that while the sun moves, the earth stands perfectly still, with magnetic north at its center and heaven about 4,000 miles above.

14

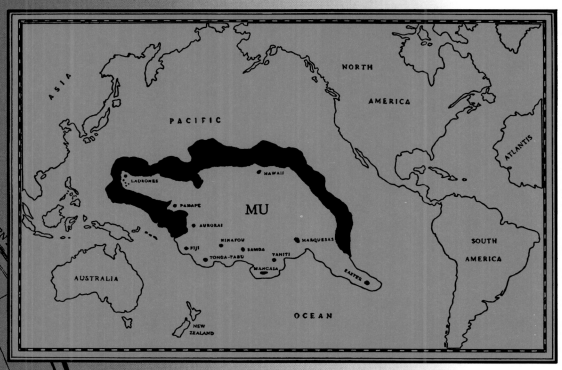

Earthquakes are said to have shattered Mu, the supposed mother of all learning, commerce, and civilization, 12,000 years ago. The Pacific engulfed the pieces, leaving only the scattered islands known today.

Atlantis was said to lie between America (to the right on this old map with north at the bottom) and the Pillars of Hercules, or Gibraltar (left). The land reportedly vanished in a great earthquake and flood that devastated Athens as well.

CHAPTER 1

Restless Spirits

lexander Tewnion, a Scottish mountaineer on leave from wartime duties, was climbing alone in the Cairngorms, rugged mountains in northeast Scotland, in October of 1943. Rations were short, so Tewnion had taken along a revolver to shoot small game for his meals. One afternoon, some days into the trek, he reached the 4,296-foot summit of Ben Macdhui. Far below, the waters of Loch Etchachan glinted in the autumn light. In the distance rose a peak known as the Black Pinnacle of Braeriach. Then, as often happens in the Cairngorms, the panorama vanished in a sudden, enveloping mist. The sky darkened and the wind picked up. Tewnion, not wanting to be caught on Macdhui's barren plateau in a storm, set off at a brisk pace.

As he tramped over the rugged scree, he suddenly heard what sounded like footsteps, spaced at long intervals, much longer than his own strides—the steps of a giant. His hand went to the loaded revolver in his pocket. Years later, in an article for the *Scots Magazine,* he described what happened next: "I peered about in the mist here rent and tattered by eddies of wind," he wrote. "A strange shape loomed up, receded, came charging at me!" Whipping out the revolver, Tewnion fired three times at the figure, but the shape kept coming. "I turned and hared down the path," he confessed, "reaching Glen Derry in a time I have never bettered."

Tewnion's panicked descent from Ben Macdhui was not the first to be reported. Half a century earlier, in 1891, a professor of chemistry at the University of London and renowned climber named Norman Collie had apparently been spurred to flight by a similar sound while on Ben Macdhui. Like Tewnion, Collie had been coming down from the summit of the mountain, moving through a dense mist. "I began to think I heard something else than merely the noise of my own footsteps," he later recalled. "For every few steps I took I heard a crunch, then another crunch, as if someone was walking after me but taking steps three or four times the length of my own."

Collie walked on, trying to dismiss the noise as "nonsense," he said, but as the eerie crunching continued, "I was seized with terror and took to my heels, staggering blindly among the boulders for four or five miles, nearly down to Rothiemurchus Forest." He could find no explanation for the event. "Whatever you make of it I do not know," he concluded, "but there is something very queer about the top of Ben Macdhui and I will not go back there again by myself."

Indeed, many say they sense a spirit on the mountain. Some claim to have seen the phantom, describing a gigantic, gray, not quite human figure. Locally, he is known as the Big Gray Man—Am Fear Liath Mór in Gaelic—and one story has it that the apparition is the ghost of a local poet who once wrote that he would "come again." More often, those who describe a strange experience on Ben Macdhui sense an unseen presence, sometimes accompanied by footsteps or the sound of unintelligible speech. Those who sense the phantom are often overcome by intense fear.

Whatever the source of the dread and the other odd manifestations atop Ben Macdhui, the uncanny phenomena give the summit a uniquely sinister reputation among Britain's peaks. Yet if researchers of the unexplained are to be believed, the world is full of such places—mountains, lakes, rivers, castles, and cities with powerful paranormal associations. Thirty miles from Ben Macdhui, for example, the famous Scottish lake known as Loch Ness supposedly holds a huge monster, a controversial claim shared by a surprising number of cold-water lakes around the globe. Not far south, ancient English burial mounds and standing stones attract psychical researchers and modern Druids.

Across the Channel, several European cities where alchemy once flourished still preserve occult monuments said to encode arcane secrets that include the keys to eternal life. And other supposedly mystical or powerful sites are to be found on every continent, from Australia to Africa to South and North America. In fact, as the maps throughout this volume indicate—and as the text documents—there are few areas of the world where a traveler is not within reach of a place that, for one reason or another, is considered a source and focus of mystery.

In all this uncanny geography, perhaps the most familiar—and among the most feared—locations are those houses, castles, and other places that, like Ben Macdhui, are said to be haunted by the phantoms of the dead, spirits of those who suffered or triumphed there in life. Skeptics scoff at the idea of ghosts, and perhaps no amount of circumstantial evidence can change their minds; but the sheer number of ghost encounters reported by different people in the same places over the years suggests to many that some puzzling phenomenon is at work. Moreover, many of the world's established religions, from Taoism to the Church of England, are prepared to offer formal services of exorcism to cast out unwanted phantoms—possibly another indication that in human affairs ghosts are not to be dismissed out of hand.

Some thoughtful researchers of haunting phenomena have concluded that ghosts are the spirits of real people who after death return, either as apparitions or unseen presences, to places that were of special importance to them in life. According to

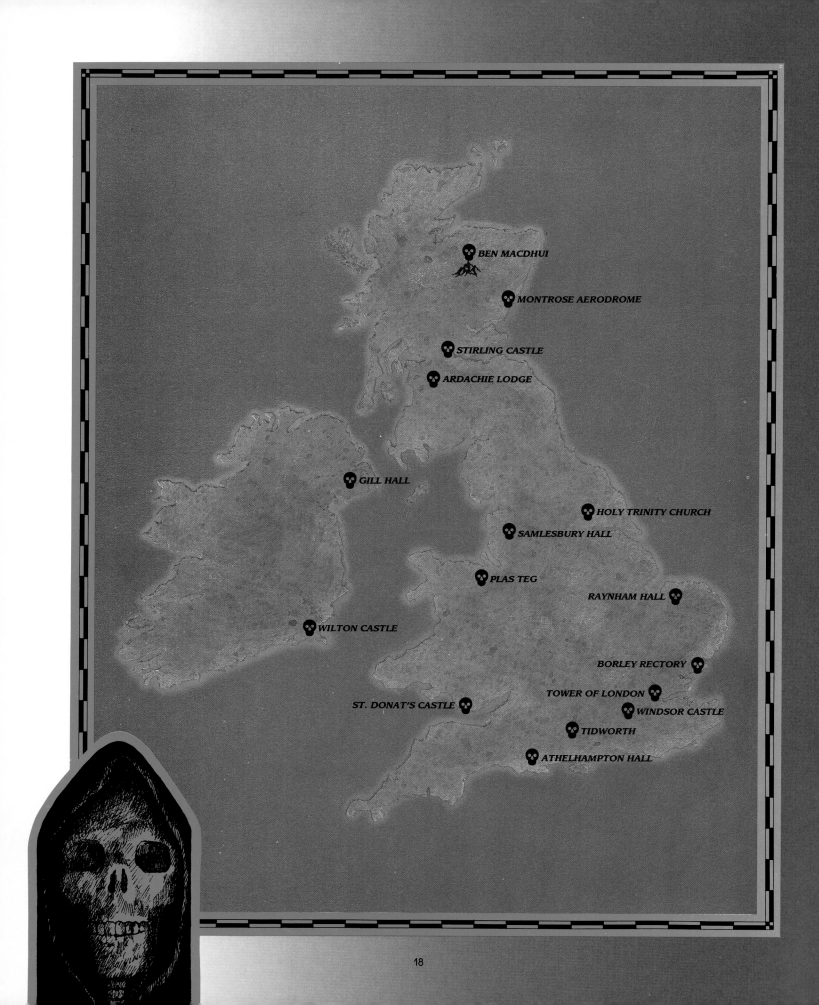

BEN MACDHUI

MONTROSE AERODROME

STIRLING CASTLE

ARDACHIE LODGE

GILL HALL

HOLY TRINITY CHURCH

SAMLESBURY HALL

PLAS TEG

RAYNHAM HALL

WILTON CASTLE

BORLEY RECTORY

ST. DONAT'S CASTLE

TOWER OF LONDON

WINDSOR CASTLE

TIDWORTH

ATHELHAMPTON HALL

this traditional view, the people who become ghosts have often participated in—or inadvertently witnessed—violence and tragedy; after death, their spirits cannot tear themselves away from the scene. A somewhat different explanation has it that highly charged human events can create fields of emotional energy strong enough to be felt in that same location years or centuries later by those with a degree of psychic perception.

Given the misty origins of the Big Gray Man, probably no one will ever know which of these theories best accounts for it—nor is it likely that doubters will ever be convinced the phantom really exists. Yet the fact that many different people at different times have claimed to per-

Warkworth Castle, Northumberland, haunted by a grieving ghost

ceive the ghost's presence is hardly startling, for few regions have such a venerable and copious tradition of haunted places as the British Isles.

Most of these hauntings are linked to specific houses, from famous castles and baronial mansions to perfectly ordinary homes in almost any town or village. But as the Scottish mountain ghost shows, not all of Britain's reputed ghosts are residential. Well to the southeast of Ben Macdhui, for example, lies Montrose Aerodrome, hard by Scotland's North Sea coast. One of the oldest military landing fields in Britain and probably the world, Montrose today is an unassuming cluster of hangars and outbuildings, some predating World War I. Yet there is nothing or-

Hauntings in the British Isles

ARDACHIE LODGE
A servant working at this house outside Glasgow, Scotland, in 1953 was driven to leave her job by what she said was a ghost that sometimes appeared as an old woman crawling across the floor toward her.

ATHELHAMPTON HALL
This Dorset manor is said to be haunted not only by several ladies and gentlemen, but also by a pet monkey that was inadvertently locked up and starved to death when its lovelorn mistress took her own life.

BEN MACDHUI
Some climbers believe this Scottish peak is haunted by more than its famous Big Gray Man. They say they have heard organ music, pipes, and unseen choirs singing on the mountain—even when no wind stirs.

BORLEY RECTORY
Centuries ago at the site of this home in Essex, England, a woman reportedly was murdered. Her ghost was then said to have haunted the place until her hidden remains were found in 1943 and properly buried.

GILL HALL
In this now-destroyed house where ghoulish noises were recorded in the 1960s, a ghost was said to have appeared in 1693 to Lady Arabella Beresford and to have accurately foretold the year of her death.

HOLY TRINITY CHURCH
Many worshipers at this church in York claim to have seen a hooded, robed phantom floating over the grounds. Some say it is the spirit of a prioress killed there for protesting Henry VIII's religious edicts.

MONTROSE AERODROME
In 1963 a man said he saw a biplane crash near this base but leave no wreckage—fifty years to the day after a young flier, whose ghost is one of two said to haunt Montrose, was killed here in a biplane crash.

PLAS TEG
This forbidding-looking mansion, built in 1610 near Mold in Wales, is supposedly haunted by two former inhabitants, both of whom committed suicide in grisly fashion after losing their beloved mates.

RAYNHAM HALL
The Brown Lady, reputed to haunt this stately home near Fakenham, was once shot at from close range by a houseguest. The bullet allegedly passed through the apparition and embedded itself in a door.

ST. DONAT'S CASTLE
A hideous winged hag reputedly haunted this seaside estate in South Glamorgan County, Wales, until the death in the mid-1700s of the last descendant of a family that had dwelt in the castle for 700 years.

SAMLESBURY HALL
The ghost of a sixteenth-century maiden is said to walk the halls and grounds of this house near Blackburn, Lancashire. Recent visitors claimed they heard sobs and witnessed the rocking of an empty chair.

STIRLING CASTLE
High above Scotland's Forth River, this stronghold—intermittent home of Mary, Queen of Scots—is said to be haunted by the ghost of the queen's handmaid. Her appearances supposedly herald disaster.

TIDWORTH
In 1661 a poltergeist reportedly wreaked havoc in the home of the justice of the peace of this village near Salisbury. So disruptive was the spirit that King Charles II dispatched an emissary to investigate the incident.

TOWER OF LONDON
Scene of countless executions, this prison is said to be as haunted as it once was bloody. Thomas à Becket, Anne Boleyn, Sir Walter Raleigh, and others supposedly wander the place in spectral form.

WILTON CASTLE
Many ghosts reportedly haunt this burned-out hulk in southeastern Ireland, once the seat of the Alcock family. The shade of Harry Alcock is said to return every December 3, the anniversary of his death in 1840.

WINDSOR CASTLE
All manner of ghosts have been reported at this British royal residence twenty miles west of London. An elderly Henry VIII supposedly signals his spectral presence with heavy groans and dragging footsteps.

dinary about the two flying phantoms said to have haunted the air base, one of them since the early 1900s.

The first of these apparitions has been identified by most accounts as the ghost of a young World War I flier named Desmond Arthur, killed when his biplane crashed in 1913 not far from the base. Three years later, according to one report, Lieutenant Arthur's disembodied figure was seen stalking the airfield five separate times by a Major Cyril Foggin and independently by several flight instructors.

The persistent phantom's most dramatic appearance, though, reportedly occurred almost twenty-five years later, during World War II, when forces based at Montrose Aerodrome were in the thick of the series of aerial engagements known as the Battle of Britain. One night in fall 1940, as the story goes, an alarm sounded at the airfield, signaling the presence of an enemy aircraft. One pilot went up in a Hurricane but after half an hour returned without having seen anything. As a ground crew watched, the Hurricane twice tried to land but inexplicably roared off just before touching down. On the third try, after the crew had lit up the landing strip with a wide-beamed searchlight, the pilot landed without incident.

As the airmen gathered near the plane, the pilot jumped out and shouted, "Who was the fool that cut me out?" When told there had been no one, the pilot was furious. "Why do you think I went round again?" he demanded. "Some madman in a biplane balked me just as I was touching down—a thing like a Tiger Moth." But no one else had been flying, the flight commander is said to have informed him. And anyway, there was no biplane at the station.

Montrose's other supposed ghostly presence dates from 1942, when a flight lieutenant crashed soon after take-off and died immediately. Before long, various people at the base began reporting they had seen the lieutenant's ghost, still clad in his flying suit and goggles. One battle-hardened veteran, arriving at the base in 1946, derided the tales on first hearing them. But one night, while on guard duty near a building that was used as the morgue, he reportedly saw the doors fly open to reveal a phantom figure, deathly white

Snow glistens on the otherwise barren heights of Scotland's Ben Macdhui (above), reputed home of an ominous presence sensed by many mountaineers. The Big Gray Man has been called a ghost, a UFO pilot, a living Buddha, and, most simply, a "spirit of the mountain."

of face, dressed in flying helmet, goggles, and full suit. The startled guard dropped his rifle and stared as the phantom headed across the field—and vanished. The doors of the morgue banged shut, and the night was once again quiet.

Thinking he might have been the butt of a joke, the pilot said nothing about the apparition. Only after the war ended and he was talking with someone who had also been stationed at Montrose did he learn that the morgue had once been a hangar—the hangar from which the flight lieutenant had emerged for his last sortie.

Montrose's haunting may not have ended with the war. In December 1987, the *Psychic News* reported that a woman driving past the field had seen an aircraft painted khaki flying so low that she could make out the rivets in the

fuselage. But the plane made absolutely no noise. She stopped the car and got out, but the plane had disappeared. She told the Montrose Aerodrome Museum Society that she thought the craft had been a World War II Spitfire or a Hurricane. The society's investigation of the airfield's history showed that a Hurricane had been among the planes that crashed at Montrose during that war.

Most of Britain's well-known haunted places are far more deeply seasoned by history than any airfield could be. For instance, Britain's castles and old stately homes seem particularly prone to attract ghosts, whether because such buildings have served as dwelling places for so many centuries, because they are a natural center of community gossip and attention, or because of the dramatic and violent events which seem to occur more frequently in those edifices than in lesser residences. In the great British houses the psychic burden of the centuries hangs heavy, and ghosts are often taken for granted—as much a part of the old homes as the very stones and timbers.

To a connoisseur of English ghosts, for example, the name Raynham Hall inevitably calls up images of the Brown Lady—a ghostly figure dressed in rich brown brocade who is said to walk the mansion's dark corridors and grand staircase. Located far south of Montrose Aerodrome and its reputed aerial phantoms, Raynham Hall stands amid the farmland of East Anglia. The hall was built in the early 1600s by Sir Roger Townshend and stayed in the Townshend family for more than 300 years. According to some accounts, its famous Brown Lady is the ghost of Dorothy Walpole, wife of Charles, the second Viscount Townshend.

Dorothy died in 1726, yet it was not until 1835 that the Brown Lady made her first recorded appearance. During the Christmas holiday in that year, a guest by the name of Colonel Loftus claimed to have glimpsed her briefly in an upstairs hall. A week later, again according to Loftus, he nearly bumped into her. Loftus said that the ghostly form he saw was dressed in brown; more disturbingly, it had no eyes—only empty sockets in a face bathed in eerie light.

Many reported sightings of the Brown Lady followed, including one by a nineteenth-century author famous for his tales of the sea, Captain Frederick Marryat, who said he encountered the Brown Lady carrying a lantern along a dark second-floor corridor.

In 1936, the phantom made its most memorable appearance. In September of that year, two photographers were hired by the then-Lady Townshend to take pictures of the house. One of them, a Captain Provand, had just finished photographing Raynham Hall's sweeping main staircase and was bent over the camera preparing the plate for the next shot. Suddenly his partner, Indre Shira, demanded that Provand take a picture of the staircase immediately—he could see a shadowy figure coming down the stairs. The startled Provand did as he was told, but scoffed at the notion that Shira had seen anything unearthly on the stairs. Yet when the film was developed, a dim figure was indeed visible, a ghostly image of a tall woman in a flowing gown.

The resulting photograph ran in that December's issue of *Country Life* and caused a sensation. Experts who examined the photograph and the plate declared that both seemed genuine. Ghostly images are easily faked by good photographers, however, so those inclined to be skeptical were not convinced.

The figure in the photograph was wearing not brown brocade but what appeared instead to be a white wedding gown. Because most reports of habitual ghosts tend to describe one particular set of clothing—be it the Brown Lady's dress or the Montrose pilot's flying suit—the discrepancy only adds to the mystery: If this was not the Brown Lady, then what was it?

For all the impressive evidence of haunting at Raynham, it is Windsor Castle that lays claim to more ghosts than any other residence in England. That claim is hardly surprising, given the history of the royal citadel, which raises its massive medieval profile above the banks of the river Thames some twenty miles west of London.

For 800 years, since the reign of William the Conqueror, British sovereigns have been born and buried within the castle's thirteen acres of gray stone buildings, vast round towers, and crenelated walls. At least four of the sovereigns—Henry VIII, his daughter Elizabeth I, the beheaded Charles I, and George III—are said to have been sighted at the castle since their deaths. A fifth ghost, that of a young guard who committed suicide in the 1920s, is also supposed to haunt the castle grounds, and a variety of other apparitions have been reported in other parts of the estate.

One of the best documented sightings of a monarch occurred in 1897, when Lieutenant Carr Glynn of the Grenadier Guards was reading in the Royal Library. Hearing the click of a woman's heels across the wooden floor, he looked up to see a tall woman in black, with a black lace veil covering her hair, come into the room, cross it, and turn right into a bay that Glynn assumed must lead into an inner room. As he was leaving the library, he mentioned the woman to the attendant, to ensure she would not inadvertently be locked in the library overnight. The attendant was puzzled: There was no inner room and upon investigation, no woman. In Queen Elizabeth I's time, however, the area had been her State Apartments. The small bay had opened onto a staircase that once led down to the terrace. The figure was thought to be the ghost of the queen, evidently drawn to the places most familiar to her in life.

Another of Windsor's reported shades, George III, made only a brief appearance some days after his death. For the last decade of his life, the unhappy monarch had suffered a form of dementia and had been confined to a suite below the Royal Library. He died there on January 29, 1820. Even in his final days, King George used to watch from his window the changing of the guard on the North Terrace below and would often wave in response to the guards' salutes as they passed. A few days after the king's death, while his body lay in state in another part of the castle, the officer in charge of the patrol, one William Knollys, glanced up at the window and according to his later account saw King George's unmistakable figure. The young officer automatically gave the command "Eyes right!" and it is said the figure raised its hand in the late king's customary response.

Psychic researcher and author Joan Forman has characterized that reported sighting as a clear case of "immediate, post-death appearance, when the surviving consciousness appears to be still attached to its old habitat, not yet adjusted to its new terms and conditions of being." In Forman's view, such a "single-appearance ghost" belongs in a different category from what she calls "regular haunters," ghosts that have been reported by different people at different times, but always in or near the same place.

Among the "regular haunters" of England's stately homes is a particular type generally known as Gray Ladies, for the color of their clothing. Not far from the city of Liverpool, in the northern English county of Lancashire, a Gray Lady is said to haunt a massive fourteenth-century mansion known as Samlesbury Hall. This well-known apparition is believed to be that of the long-dead Dorothy Southworth, daughter of Sir John Southworth, a former owner of the hall.

In the 1500s, the story goes, Dorothy fell in love with the son of a neighboring family. Although the family was prosperous it was also Protestant, which enraged Sir John, a stout Catholic. He forbade the two to marry—and so, in time-honored fashion, the young couple decided to elope. But one of Dorothy's brothers overheard their plans and laid a deadly ambush to preserve his family's pride.

Tradition has it he killed the groom-to-be and two of the unlucky suitor's friends, burying the bodies in secret near the hall. Dorothy was sent abroad, consigned in disgrace to a convent, where she is said to have gone mad and died. (Three centuries later, workers building a new road alongside the walls of the hall found a grisly confirmation of at least part of the story: a grave with three skeletons.)

Such circumstances might be said to be an ideal blueprint for a haunting by the would-be bride, and Samlesbury Hall is indeed well known for the ghostly woman who is

Exuding a ghostly atmosphere in the eerie photograph above, England's Raynham Hall was said to be a house of sorrows for its best-known occupant, Dorothy Walpole. Brought here as an unwilling bride, she was reportedly held prisoner for years by a lecherous, possessive husband before dying mysteriously in 1726. Legend says she was discovered with her neck broken at the foot of Raynham's grand staircase—only a few steps from where the vapory female form at right, identified by many as her ghost, was photographed in 1936.

said to be seen moving through its corridors and out into the grounds. During World War II, she was reportedly encountered by soldiers quartered nearby, and in the 1970s, a bus driver on the main road is said to have stopped to let her come aboard. In 1981 another driver claimed that when passing the hall at about 4:30 a.m. with a load of fruit he had had to slam on his brakes when the ghostly figure of a woman in a flowing gown drifted in front of his truck.

Not all supposed British ghosts are as sweetly sad as Dorothy and other English Gray Ladies, however. Some 150 miles from Samlesbury Hall, across the broad Irish Sea, the mansion of Gill Hall apparently housed a far more robust phantom until fairly recently. A three-story structure overlooking extensive parklands, Gill Hall was built by one John Magill near Dromore in County Down of Northern Ireland in the 1670s. In its time the house was said to have a ghost or two of a fairly conventional variety. Then, in the twentieth century, what seemed to be new ghostly presences appeared, marking their arrival with loud, unexplained noises.

As later reported by Sheila St. Clair, a British psychic investigator, the modern manifestations at Gill Hall seemed more in the line of poltergeists than apparitions. For purists in ghostly matters, poltergeists are concentrations of mischievous or malevolent energy, more likely to be associated with people than places. Yet some reported poltergeists—like the one at Gill Hall—seem to be more like other ghosts in their strong attachment to specific locations.

In June of 1961, St. Clair said, she was asked by a group called the Ulster Tape Recording Society to help investigate some strange noises the group had earlier taperecorded at Gill Hall, which had then been abandoned and deteriorating for about twenty years. Members of the group were also interested in explaining why the supposedly empty mansion should have made them all feel so uneasy.

On a midsummer evening, the group placed microphones in various rooms of the hall and wired them to tape recorders. St. Clair and the others planned to stay in a large room on the ground floor and listen to whatever the remote microphones picked up. At 11:45 p.m., according to St. Clair's account, some uncanny phenomena began. The doors of the room designated as the listening post—heavy doors that normally swung only a few inches and stopped, even with a hard push—opened by themselves and swung back to the wall. Then, at 11:50, pandemonium erupted in

In a vivid depiction on the pub sign (below) of New Hall Tavern in Samlesbury, Lancashire, the ghost of Dorothy Southworth steals across the grounds of her old home, Samlesbury Hall.

Along with the British monarchs said to haunt Windsor Castle (above, left) are the alleged ghosts of several royal servants. One of them, King Richard II's huntsman (left), supposedly gallops through nearby Windsor Great Park to foretell national disasters.

the other rooms. The microphones in the cellar relayed a series of loud crashes, followed by an incredible roaring sound that St. Clair described as "a cross between the sound of roaring flames and a beast-like noise."

Over the next two hours, most of the din seemed to come from the cellar. But if anyone ventured down the stairs to investigate, all noise instantly stopped, according to St. Clair, "and there was a kind of heavy brooding silence" that made them feel they were being watched. When the investigators returned to the control room the racket started up again, reaching an intensity between 2:00 a.m. and 3:00 a.m. that St. Clair called "astounding." Near dawn, the cacophony coming through the speakers diminished, and with the first streaks of light it ceased altogether. The weary group packed up and went home.

Later, replays of the tapes revealed that whenever the investigators were moving around the house, their echoing footsteps produced some distortion on the tapes, described in one account as "howl-back." But none of the unexplained noises—crashes, indistinct muttering, gongs, chiming clocks, footsteps on the stairs—suffered any such effects; indeed, St. Clair declared, "they might have been taped in a soundproof studio." The technical engineers were baffled. The group also had no explanation for their sense of being watched or for feeling so cold that, despite the balmy evening, many of them had put on coats and parkas. The mystery may never be solved, for in June 1970 the derelict hall somehow caught fire and burned to the ground. Its charred shell, deemed unsafe, was later blown up. With the destruction of Gill Hall, the mansion's unsettled spirit or spirits apparently departed. To date, no more phantom encounters have been reported at the building's old site.

The British Isles' rich tradition of haunted castles and homes has influenced perceptions of ghost phenomena in fact and fiction around the world, but the British Isles certainly have no monopoly on ghosts. The Americas boast an abundant roster of durable spirits reputed to abide in specific locations important to them in life, eerie sites where they variously terrify, puzzle, or fascinate the humans who remain behind. By and large, New World hauntings tend to be of more recent vintage—but for those who encounter them, the ghosts of the Americas are no less powerful or bizarre than the many reported British phantoms.

In the eastern Canadian province of Nova Scotia, for example, an isolated farmhouse was allegedly the scene of a particularly virulent poltergeist visitation in 1922 that received intense local press coverage at the time. Caledonia Mills in Guysborough County, about a hundred miles from the capital of Halifax, was the home of seventy-year-old Alexander MacDonald, his wife, Mary, and their sixteen-year-old adopted daughter Mary Ellen.

The trouble reportedly began on the morning of Saturday, January 7, 1922, when Mr. MacDonald went downstairs and found unexplained ashes on top of the kitchen stove and on the floor. Investigation showed that loose boards in the ceiling near the stovepipe had been burning, even though there was no fire in the stove at the time. The next night, Mrs. MacDonald woke to the smell of smoke and the crackling of burning wood. Her husband's rapid search uncovered five separate fires in the loft above the kitchen. The fires returned the next night, this time in the upholstery of a rocking chair and a couch.

By now the family was thoroughly alarmed and called in some neighbors to help. In the course of that day and the next night, the MacDonalds and their neighbors put out thirty-one blazes, in all parts of the house. The following day, the beleaguered family moved out.

But that was not the end. Two detectives decided to investigate the weird events by staying in the house. Nothing happened the first night, but the following evening they reported they heard the sound of someone walking in the room at the top of the stairs and then coming down the stairway. After they went to sleep, each claimed later, they were awakened by someone or something punching them in the arm. Searches upstairs and down revealed nothing.

Despite that somewhat inconclusive investigation, some people in the region maintained that the teenager, Mary Ellen, must be the responsible agent, at least in the case of the earlier fires. Perhaps, they said, she was simply bored with life on the isolated farm. But others pointed out that some of the fires had broken out in the house when Mary Ellen was at least a mile away. For their part, the two detectives agreed that the fires and the strange incidents that occurred during their visit to the house had a shared supernatural origin and were not caused by human agency. The two offered a $100 reward to anyone who could prove otherwise within a year.

On May 7, 1922, the MacDonalds tried to move back into their battered home, but that same afternoon another fire broke out upstairs. Fed up, the family promptly moved out again, this time for good. In time, the elderly MacDonalds died, and Mary Ellen moved to Ontario, where she married and raised a family. The mystery of Caledonia Mills and its seemingly restless spirit was never fully solved.

In the western Massachusetts town of Lenox, several hundred miles southwest of Nova Scotia and a world re-

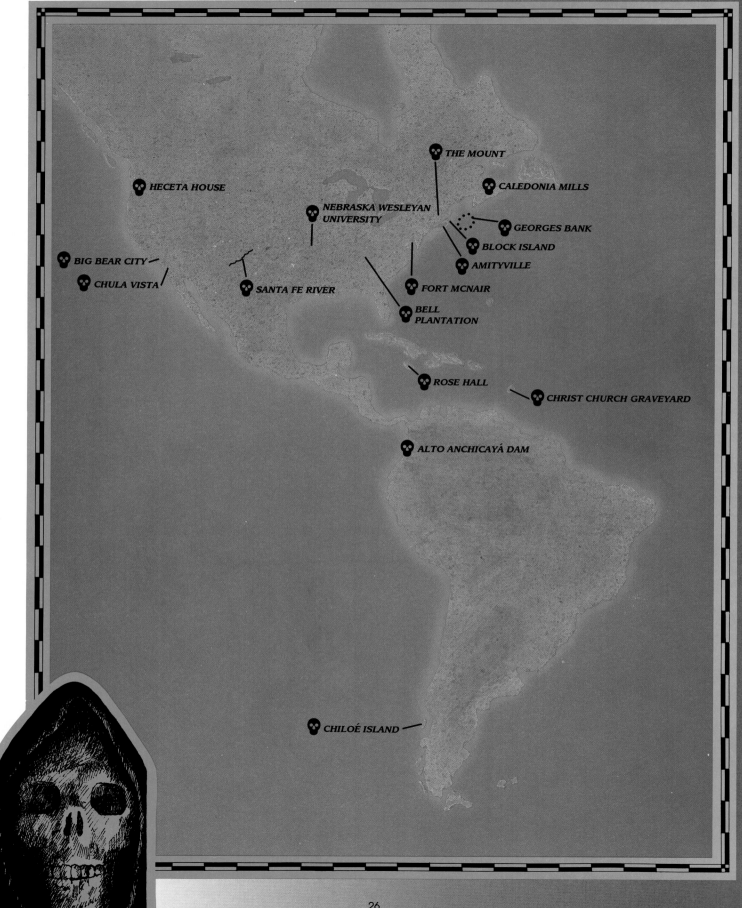

THE MOUNT

CALEDONIA MILLS

HECETA HOUSE

NEBRASKA WESLEYAN
UNIVERSITY

GEORGES BANK

BLOCK ISLAND

BIG BEAR CITY

AMITYVILLE

CHULA VISTA

SANTA FE RIVER

FORT MCNAIR

BELL
PLANTATION

ROSE HALL

CHRIST CHURCH GRAVEYARD

ALTO ANCHICAYÁ DAM

CHILOÉ ISLAND

26

moved from the MacDonalds' modest farmhouse, stands The Mount, a neo-Georgian mansion built for novelist Edith Wharton at the beginning of the twentieth century. The Mount, like Caledonia Mills, has reportedly seen its share of phantom activity. But here the ghostly inhabitants seem to be kindly relics from the past, unlikely to threaten harm to those with whom they share the house today.

Edith Wharton used the estate as a country retreat and became deeply attached to it. Although she sold the property a few years after her permanent departure from the United States in 1908 and had no further association with it before her death in 1937, tradition and some eyewitness accounts suggest that after death Wharton and a

Heceta House, on Oregon's lonely coast

few of her friends have returned to the house in which she had been happiest.

After Wharton's death, the property passed through the hands of various owners, including Foxhollow School, a girls' boarding school that used The Mount as a dormitory. Stories of ghosts were rampant there, according to alumna Dorothy Carpenter, who was interviewed on the subject in the mid-1980s. "Every time we'd hear a squeak, we'd say it was Edith Wharton's ghost," Carpenter said. "But nobody really thought it was." Some years later, other incidents caused Carpenter to change her mind.

After Foxhollow stopped using The Mount, it began to deteriorate, and in the early 1970s Carpenter took it upon

Phantoms of the Americas

ALTO ANCHICAYÁ DAM
The few who live near this dam thirty miles west of Cali, Colombia, say the area abounds with ghosts—including a hitchhiking male phantom and the shade of a one-legged woman that preys on anyone alone.

AMITYVILLE
In 1975 a couple bought a house in this Long Island town only to be terrorized, they said, by "unseen forces." Their story became a popular book and movie, spurring charges that it was a moneymaking hoax.

BELL PLANTATION
A crude, abusive spirit reportedly tormented Bell family members on this cotton farm in Tennessee between 1817 and 1821. The ghost allegedly attacked the children and killed the father by poisoning.

BIG BEAR CITY
In 1962 a family named Lowe fled their home in this southern California town after it was pelted with rocks and pebbles over a four-month period. A psychical investigator claimed a poltergeist caused the barrage.

BLOCK ISLAND
A ghost ship, deck and sails ablaze, is said to haunt the seas off this island in Long Island Sound. Allegedly plundered and burned by wreckers in 1752, the spectral ship was reported seen as recently as 1969.

CALEDONIA MILLS
Just before mysterious fires drove the MacDonalds from their home in this Nova Scotia town, a witness said the house was "strangely illuminated, as sudden and bright as a short circuit on a high tension wire."

CHILOÉ ISLAND
A phantom ship is said to haunt this Chilean island's waters and to abduct the living. Locals say one man returned demented after fifty years, and another gone only two days came back with a huge chest scar.

CHRIST CHURCH GRAVEYARD
Coffins in a vault in this cemetery outside Bridgetown, Barbados, reportedly shifted about inexplicably in the early 1800s until the governor ordered the coffins to be buried elsewhere and the vault abandoned.

CHULA VISTA
When people in this San Diego suburb claimed to see the face of a murdered nine-year-old girl in the shadows on a blank billboard, the news drew huge crowds, hot dog vendors, and a two-mile-long traffic jam.

FORT MCNAIR
At this Washington, D.C., army post, Mary Surratt was hanged—unjustly, some say— as a conspirator in the Lincoln assassination. Her spirit is said to walk the fort in hanging clothes, her neck broken.

GEORGES BANK
During a gale one night in 1869, two schooners collided in this North Atlantic fishing ground. The Andrew Jackson sank, but the other ship survived, reportedly to be haunted by ghosts of the Jackson's crew.

HECETA HOUSE
Residents and guests at this former lighthouse keeper's house on Oregon's coast have reported a female ghost peering in windows, floating through closed doors, and emitting bloodcurdling screams.

THE MOUNT
Novelist Edith Wharton built this mansion in Massachusetts around 1900. Subsequent residents said they saw ghosts of Wharton and her companions; one woman even exchanged nods with the dead writer.

NEBRASKA WESLEYAN UNIVERSITY
One day in 1963, a secretary at this school in Lincoln entered a room and felt she had walked into the past. She saw a woman in archaic dress and a century-old pastoral scene where the street should have been.

ROSE HALL
In 1952, psychic Eileen Garrett visited the ruins of this allegedly haunted house in Montego Bay, Jamaica. She is said to have contacted and pacified the spirit of the house's cruel and corrupt former mistress.

SANTA FE RIVER
Along this and other rivers in the Southwest, the spirit of La Llorona, or Weeping Woman, is said to walk, mourning for her two young sons who drowned because of her neglect.

The happy ghost of author Edith Wharton is said to visit The Mount (below), her rural Massachusetts home. Although Wharton (right) lived there no more than five years before she moved to France in 1908, the mansion remained one of her favorite places on earth.

herself to preserve the ornate ceiling in the ballroom. For two months she lived there alone. Then one day, she said, "I saw a ghost on the terrace." Carpenter described the apparition as wearing a summery, off-white dress, "maybe lace but not real gauzy." She instantly identified the ghost as that of Edith Wharton, recognizing her from pictures. The apparition seemed alive, Carpenter said. It walked along the terrace, approached the edge, and walked back.

A few years later, members of an acting troupe called Shakespeare & Company, which moved into The Mount in 1978, also reported having felt the presence of Wharton—and of some other spirits as well. One evening during the winter of 1979, actress and voice teacher Andrea Haring decided to sleep in what had once been Wharton's writing room, now bare of furniture except for a spare mattress. "I stoked up the wood stove in the room," she later explained, "so that it should have stayed warm until about noon the next day." But at four in the morning, she awoke because the room had gone freezing cold.

She sensed someone else was present, Haring later recalled, and when she opened her eyes, she saw three people. One figure she recognized as Edith Wharton. Haring also said she saw a man with muttonchops writing at a table, and she thought she recognized the third figure as Wharton's husband Edward, or Teddy, whom the author divorced at about the time she left The Mount and went to Europe. After a few minutes, Haring steeled herself to get up and leave the room. "As I closed the door," she said, "I still saw them there." When she returned a little later, however, the formerly frigid room was warm again and the phantom trio was gone.

The next day Haring saw a book full of photographs of people Wharton had known, and found the identity of the man she hadn't recognized: "It turned out to be a guy who they suspected was Edith Wharton's lover and who had also helped her in a secretarial way in some of her works." Haring's conclusion regarding her experience was that "past, present, and future were all happening at the same time, that for some reason time as we know it was irrelevant."

While The Mount may be inhabited by spirits of people who were fond of the place, Fort Lesley J. McNair, on the banks of the Potomac River in Washington, D.C., is reputed to be haunted by, among other alleged phantoms, the ghost of one who felt her life was unjustly ended there. In 1865, Mary Surratt was convicted of conspiracy in the assassination of President Abraham Lincoln by John Wilkes Booth. Fort McNair served as a holding site for Surratt and the others convicted with her as they awaited execution.

On July 7, Surratt, a strapping widow who had run the boardinghouse where the conspirators met, was led with the others to a set of gallows that had been built in the courtyard of the fort specifically for the execution of the guilty crew. If the sentence were carried out, Surratt would become the first woman ever executed by the federal government. Even the hangman later said that a commuted sentence for Surratt seemed likely right up to the end. But the message of mercy never came.

Supported on either side by soldiers and barely able to walk, Surratt went up the final steps. With the noose adjusted around her neck, the one-time boardinghouse landlady could see the coffin and open grave that awaited her. "Don't let me fall," she begged—and then the floor dropped out from beneath her feet, her neck snapped, and she was dead.

At the time, some contended that judgment had been rushed and that Surratt, in particular, was innocent. Should that charge be true, it is no wonder that Surratt's ghost is said to linger. According to one account, published in the *Washington Post* in 1991, army captain David Osborne reported that on Lincoln's birthday in 1989 he heard what he believed was the voice of Mary Surratt outside his window. "It started off softly crying, 'Help me, help me,'" he said.

"Then she began screaming, 'Oh no, help me, help me.'" When he raced outside, no one was there.

Erik Swanson, a young honor guard officer at Fort McNair, also told the *Post* of an eerie phenomenon, which he claimed to have witnessed more than once while on duty: A path two feet wide and about 300 yards long would simply and suddenly appear in snow up to twelve inches deep, melting the snow right down to bare grass. Swanson swore there were no pipes belowground along the path, that no one had dug it out, and that there was nothing else to explain its presence—except that, as he learned, the path coincided exactly with the route of Mary Surratt's final, halting passage from her cell to the waiting gallows.

In addition to haunting Fort McNair, Mary Surratt's ghost was once said to frequent her old boardinghouse on H Street, a few miles away. Later inhabitants reported hearing mysterious footsteps in empty rooms, which some attributed to Surratt's restless spirit looking for justice. Others thought she was simply checking up on the place.

Such domestic tendencies seem to be a common thread of house hauntings. Indeed, another notable American haunted house, clear across the country from the nation's capital, is also said to house the ghost of a woman—in this case, name unknown—who apparently maintains a

Moments before Mary Surratt (right) was hanged at Fort McNair (below), the Lincoln assassination conspirator next to her on the gallows declared, "Mrs. Surratt is innocent. She doesn't deserve to die." Some say her wrongful execution causes her to haunt the fort.

watchful eye on her former home. The dwelling, and the lighthouse it was built to accompany, are located atop rugged, green Heceta Head, which juts into the Pacific Ocean a few miles north of the Oregon coastal town of Florence. Built in the late nineteenth century, Heceta House is now owned by the Forest Service.

In 1979 the caretakers of Heceta House, Harry and Ann Tammen, told an interviewer several stories of seemingly paranormal encounters with a ghostly, withered old woman. The Tammens, who had moved into the house in 1973, referred to the apparition as Rue, a name that was spelled out one night on a Ouija board, and added that there is speculation that Rue was a lighthouse keeper's wife whose baby died and was buried at home. Indeed, an old photo of the house shows a tombstone in the front lawn. Whatever her identity in life, Rue seemed to have retained an interest in the upkeep of Heceta House after death.

According to the Tammens, Rue has appeared to several people. Perhaps the most dramatic encounter involved a local contractor named Jim Alexander, who was hired by the Forest Service to make some repairs on the house. One job was to mend a broken window in the attic, which was reached through a trapdoor in the ceiling of the Tammens' bedroom below. Having hoisted himself into the attic, Alexander was working on the window when he suddenly saw the reflection of someone in the glass.

He turned around and found himself face to face with a very old, wrinkled woman, wearing what he described as "pioneer-type clothes." As Alexander told the Tammens afterward, "the first thing I noticed was, she's coming towards me but she's not taking steps. She's floating." Apparently the apparition's dress ended about six inches from the floor, and there were no feet to be seen.

As the figure drew nearer, the terrified Alexander plunged past it—later, he said he may actually have passed through it—and jumped, feet first, through the trapdoor. The Tammens, sitting in the kitchen directly beneath their bedroom, were startled by the sound of the builder's crashlanding, then heard him run out the front door, slam the

A Face on a Billboard

When nine-year-old Laura Arroyo *(inset)* vanished from her San Diego home in June 1991, her family and friends could only hope for her safe return. Sixteen hours later, their hopes were cruelly dashed when the child was found murdered. Grief turned to fear and anger as the killer remained at large.

According to many, those feelings may have been shared by Arroyo's troubled spirit, because the next month, in the nearby town of Chula Vista where her body had been discovered, people began believing they saw the child's face on a blank billboard. The ghostly image appeared at night, in the form of subtle shadows on the floodlit expanse of the board *(right)*.

As word of the phenomenon spread, viewers from all over the San Diego area made their way to the billboard's location at the corner of Broadway and Main Street. Huge traffic jams developed as crowds swelled to as many as 20,000 people in a single night—stopping, peering, pointing out to companions *(lower right)* the supposed features of the little girl.

The board's owners put in brighter lights to eliminate the shadows, but people still saw an image. When the company tried turning off the lights, a faulty timing device turned them back on. Finally, the owners removed the bulbs altogether, plunging the board into darkness. Nonetheless, visitors to the place reported that they could still sense Arroyo's presence. "You can't see it," said one, "but you can feel it."

door of his truck, and speed away. "We never did get an explanation till a day or two later," Harry Tammen said, "when he came back to get his tools."

About a week afterward, the Tammens were awakened at night by the sound of sweeping. "It was a broom on the old wood floor of the attic," Harry Tammen said, "and you'd hear the little tinkle of the glass." Alexander had departed in such haste that he had left the broken window glass from his repair job scattered on the floor, but when Harry went upstairs the next morning, he found the glass neatly swept into a pile. Covering the floor were tracks such as might be made by an old-fashioned hearth broom.

The Tammens, like Andrea Haring at The Mount, have advanced the tentative theory that the apparition at Heceta House is evidence of a kind of temporal displacement allowing the interaction of past and present at the same point in space. While telling their interviewer they "don't, per se, believe in ghosts," as Harry Tammen put it, "we wonder if there isn't a little short circuit in time."

As in Britain, not all ghosts in the Americas are linked to houses or even military barracks like Fort McNair. One unusual South American example is the Alto Anchicayá Dam, built between the Anchicayá and Verde rivers in Colombia. Located deep in the jungle about thirty miles west of Cali, the Alto Anchicayá Dam is said to be the site of far more unhappy hauntings than those of the gentle, airborne Rue of Heceta Head. Some sixty workers died during the dam's hazardous construction between 1970 and 1974, and many locals believe the ghosts of those men travel the area.

Among the more detailed accounts of such hauntings is the story told by Craig Downer, a native of Carson Valley, Nevada, and a Peace Corps volunteer, who spent some time in the small community of Yatacue below the dam in 1978. Part of Downer's job was to take an inventory of the vertebrate species to be found in a nearby national park, and he often made nighttime collecting excursions.

One night in June of 1978, Downer wrote in an account published four years later, he and Gerardo Cortezar, a young helper, were poking along a roadside ditch and nearby bushes. Downer noticed the dim yellow lights of what he took to be a pickup truck approaching from the dam; he was mildly puzzled when the lights disappeared and the truck never came past them on the road. The two men continued on, and after several minutes, Downer glanced down the road and was stunned by what he saw. Coming toward him, as he wrote later, was "a bright, quavering, luminous cloud in the shape of a man."

The apparition seemed to be communicating ill will and what Downer later described as "a horrible, hellish despair, a malignancy which gave me the shudders yet at the same time fascinated me." The form floated closer, according to Downer's account, as both men stood transfixed. Finally, when it was within about sixty feet, Downer drew his machete and signaled Cortezar to get going. The two bolted back up the road, feeling, Downer wrote, "as if some presence were watching us and trying to draw us back."

Downer made no more nocturnal excursions and for a

time told no one about the experience. Then one day he learned about a fatal accident that had occurred there a few years earlier during the dam's construction. A pickup truck carrying workers on the project had rolled over the edge of the road, hitting the riverbank and killing the worker on the passenger's side instantly; the driver had been paralyzed from the waist down. Since then others were said to have reported seeing a spirit at the site of the accident.

Downer immediately recalled his own ghostly encounter. He had seen faint headlights and had expected a truck to pass them on the road, but it hadn't. "At the time I thought the vehicle had parked and turned off its headlights," Downer wrote. "Now I believe it was an apparition and the whole episode a ghostly reenactment of the horrible accident. I believe the man who was killed dwells at this spot, unable to escape or to face the fact that he is dead. He frequently reenacts the tragedy and is caught up in some hellish state which gives him no peace. This is the horror I felt, as if the apparition had communicated it to me."

Far to the south of Cali's isolated dam site, beyond the rugged Andes mountains, Chiloé Island slumbers off Chile's Pacific coast. It is a big island, 150 miles long and 30 miles wide, with two main towns and many fishing villages bounded by dense forests. From seaward, Chiloé probably looks much as it did more than four centuries ago when the ship *Caleuche* is said to have first made a landfall on the island. That was in the time of the conquistadors, but some residents of Chiloé firmly believe that the *Caleuche* still sails these Pacific waters and still visits Chiloé.

Late one night in 1968, for example, a local pastor named Aaron Garcia Gonzalez was convinced he saw the *Caleuche* enter the waters of the Rio Pudeto, a shallow, unnavigable river that lay near his home. According to one account, Garcia said he saw "several brilliant lights, then a mast, then two more masts, and finally a ship illuminated in brilliant colors." After half an hour, he said, the ship disappeared as slowly as it had materialized.

Skeptics consider the *Caleuche* merely a bit of folklore that exists only in the vivid imaginations of the islanders—and it is true that many islanders regard the ghost ship and its magical crew as a colorful part of their culture, something that distinguishes them from mainland Chileans.

Yet for those who say they have seen the ghost ship, such as Graciela Ruiz, a seamstress on the island of Lemuy, the sightings are very real. One night in 1976, Ruiz later recalled, she and some friends hid behind rocks on a hill overlooking the bay, apparently hoping to glimpse the ghost ship. At midnight, she said, "we saw a light rising from the depths of the water and it lit up the entire bay. A gigantic ship emerged, bright as gold." For four hours, Ruiz and her friends allegedly watched men and women dancing in a huge salon on board, while the strains of the orchestral music drifted across the water. When the first streaks of dawn appeared, the ship started to sink. "We watched until it vanished beneath the surface," Ruiz said. "Only then could we leave because it would have been dangerous before."

Beyond the Americas—and the ghost-infested British Isles—lies a world of reputedly haunted sites. A tour of such ghostly scenes would be ambitious indeed, for there is hardly a region of the globe that does not have its phantom-infested houses, castles, and other sites. Many of the reported hauntings take the familiar forms of the poltergeist, the victim of violence, or the otherwise restless soul. But others are seen through the lenses of local tradition. The basic fact of haunting, if indeed it is a reality, may be the same, but the explanations for it sometimes vary from country to country, culture to culture.

In the rural parts of Norway, for example, the borders between places may be haunted by a quintessentially Norwegian ghost known as a *deildegast,* a spirit doomed to spend eternity returning to the scene of its crime. *Deilde,* in Norwegian, are boundary stones, and *gast* means ghost (as does the German *Geist).* The deildegast is, accordingly, the unhappy spirit of a man who tried in life to cheat his neighbors by surreptitiously moving the stones—an unforgivable crime. The phantom's dreary fate is to try, but forever fail, to find the stones he moved and make good the damage. Although rarely reported today, deildegasts were once said to stalk the countryside of Norway, clad in long coats, blue stockings, and large shoes, accosting the living to ask for help in their hopeless quest.

Across the cold Norwegian Sea in Iceland, stories tell of an equally chilly phantom with a more familiar origin. Tales of the ghost known as Skerflod-Mori date from the late 1700s. He is said to have been the ghost of a traveler who drowned on a terrible winter night and who then for many years terrorized the nearby town of Stokkseyri. His favorite victims were the descendants of the man who had refused him shelter on that bitter night and so caused his death, but the icy phantom also wreaked mischief on travelers, farmers, and fishermen throughout the region.

In the winter and spring of 1892, Skerflod-Mori is said to have haunted a number of huts near the sea, where the crews of fishing boats slept. For six weeks that season, a willful presence seemed to bedevil the huts, afflicting the men's dreams, preventing sleep, and inflicting physical

Said to prowl the ocean near Chile's Chiloé Island, the phantom sailing ship Caleuche glows with light in the painting below, which reflects the belief that the ghostly crew hold brightly lit revels on board. Some accounts say the ship's phantom crew may take the shape of wolves, fish, rocks, and birds, as well as humans. It is said that anyone who causes them harm, even unwittingly, runs the risk of sailing the seas forever as a galley slave.

Rodenstein Castle, in the Eberbach Valley near Heidelberg, Germany

Ghosts around the Globe

BÉLMEZ
In the 1970s, images of human faces appeared mysteriously on a floor in a home in this village near Córdoba, Spain. Spirits from an old graveyard under the house were said to have caused the ghostly portraits.

CARINI CASTLE
Sicilians say that the beautiful Baroness Carini, killed here by her father in 1563, left a bloody hand print which remained visible, despite scrubbing and painting, until the wall it was on collapsed some decades ago.

DJAJAPURA
Target of a 1944 Allied assault, this northern New Guinea port—then called Hollandia—was said to be haunted for more than a decade afterward by the spirits of Japanese soldiers at an antiaircraft gun.

EBERBACH VALLEY
The clatter of a spectral army over this German valley, said to signal war's onset or end, was reported just before Germany's 1945 defeat. Many such reports may make these the world's best documented ghosts.

GALLIPOLI
This lonely Turkish peninsula—scene of a bloody Allied campaign of World War I—is said to be haunted by an Australian stretcher-bearer, John S. Kirkpatrick, who acted valiantly in life to save many comrades.

NYON
At a chateau now serving as a hotel in this Swiss town, the ghost of the French writer Voltaire has allegedly been sensed, and occasionally seen, in a chamber in which he frequently stayed during life.

THE OUTBACK
The ghost of an Arunta tribesman reported to haunt a clearing about 100 miles from Alice Springs would in life have been immersed in magic. Aborigine tradition attributed even death itself to the work of magicians.

PLAINS OF MARATHON
In these fields north of Athens—scene of a bloody battle in which the Athenians repelled the Persians in 490 BC—people supposedly heard the screams of the wounded and the whistle of spears for years afterward.

SAINT-QUENTIN
In 1849 a barrage of invisible projectiles pierced kitchen windows without shattering them in a home in this French town. The spirit believed responsible went away after a servant was discharged.

SCHWEIZER-RENEKE
A farmer near this South African town said he was stunned to see bread pans, flatirons, a pot, and the meat he was frying move unaided into an oven—the work, it was thought, of a pesky spirit called Old Griet.

SOUTH CHINA
In this part of the country, people burn paper boats to symbolically speed the spirits of the dead on their passage into the next world, an honor meant to prevent their return to earth as malevolent ghosts.

STOKKSEYRI
A phantom that reportedly plagued fishermen near this Icelandic town in 1892 was said to make sleeping men whimper as if in pain and those awake turn blue as they lost all strength from their limbs.

TELEMARK
Norwegian tradition says that deildegasts—ghosts of people who moved boundary stones to steal land—can be aided by living persons who meet them to hear where the stones belong and then put them there.

TOKYO
Respect for the angry ghost of a seventeenth-century woman named Oiwa, who was wronged by her husband, is indicated by her gravestone, which is four feet higher than any other in Tokyo's Aoyama cemetery.

VERSAILLES
Two women visiting this grand palace near Paris in 1901 allegedly experienced retrocognitive haunting. They claimed to have stepped for a few moments into the era of Queen Marie-Antoinette and her court.

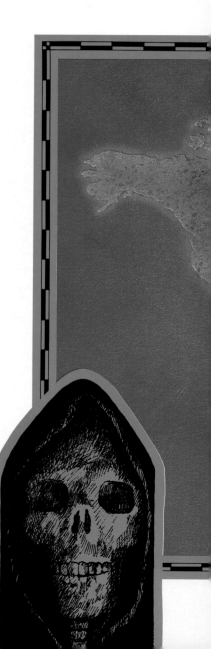

pain. Descriptions of the phantom varied. Some of the fishermen reported seeing ''a bluish cloud of vapour that moved back and forth and sometimes glowed.'' Others reportedly saw ''a lump, about the size of a small dog.'' Still others were aware of a sudden chill wind. The men of one hut borrowed the bell from the local church. The charm is said to have brought temporary relief—but to have worked in only one hut at a time.

Finally, the harrassed fishermen appealed to a man named Eyolf Magnusson, thought by the people in the district to possess a power with rhymed spells. Magnusson agreed to rid the parish of the hauntings but did not promise the cure would last forever. It is said that he uttered certain verses and sent the ghost north to another island.

One of the few phantoms said to haunt the skies—albeit in a highly localized fashion—is reputedly to be found well south and east of Iceland's icy waters in central Germany. Deep in the low, rounded mountains of the Odenwald range, northeast of Mannheim, the gloomy ruin of Rodenstein Castle rises above Eberbach Valley. There, in 1634, Marie von Hochberg, wife of the duke of Rodenstein, lay dying. During her life she had come to hate her husband for his continual warlike rampages into the countryside, and so in dying she cursed him. After his own death, she proclaimed with her final breath, he was to ride forever through the skies with his contentious entourage.

Since then, legend holds, whenever war is about to break out or end, the phantom duke and his invisible band

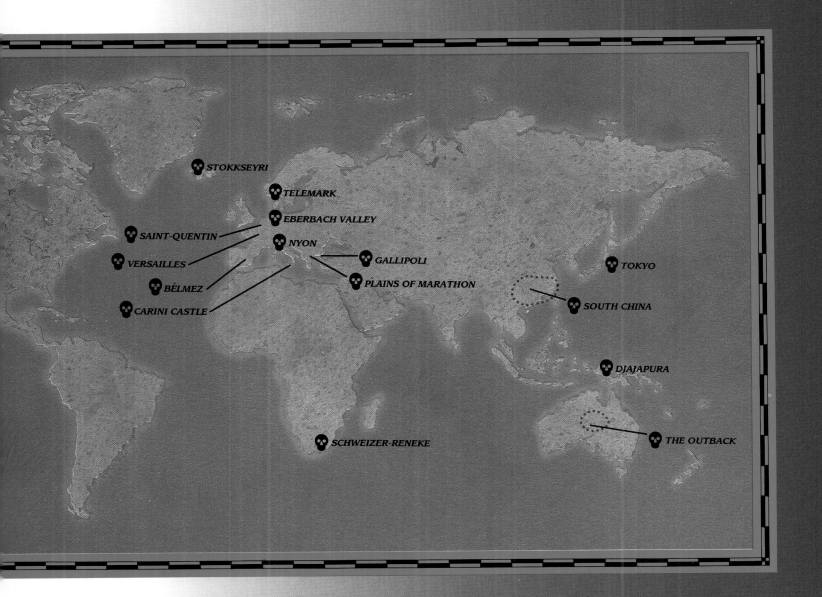

At left, the maddened samurai Iemon swings his sword at the huge, looming specter of his dead wife Oiwa, invisible to his mistress and another guest. Betrayed by her husband in life, the virtuous Oiwa is said to have taken a deadly revenge upon him and others after her premature death. Even today, her spirit is considered both wrathful and potent, and a respectful shrine, seen in the large picture at right, marks her birthplace near the imperial palace in the Yotsuya district of Tokyo. Oiwa's grave (inset), located in a prominent, tree-shaded spot in the Aoyama cemetery in the Sugamo district, is also something out of the ordinary. Its unusually large stone is surrounded by dozens of inscribed prayer sticks left by visitors, far more sticks than would be found at an ordinary Japanese tomb.

of knights, horses, and wagons are heard rattling through the sky from the ruins of Rodenstein Castle, across the Eberbach Valley to Reichenberg Castle on the other side.

The duke's ghostly rides were taken seriously enough in the mid-eighteenth century that legal experts from the Reichenberg area collected reports from local inhabitants on what was described as "a land spirit from the county Erbach." This collection, called the Reichenberg Protocol, along with later additions, chronicles the irregular sorties said to have been made by the old duke and his men. Several of the duke's reputed appearances did occur around the dates that wars began or ended. In 1871, for example, two weeks before the end of the Franco-Prussian War, Adam Blumenschein, a soldier from the area, is said to have received a letter from home reporting that the duke of Rodenstein had ridden and that peace was therefore at hand.

One day during the summer of 1914, an old woman who lived near Rodenstein Castle said she heard a mysterious humming, buzzing, and roaring. Springing from her bed, she woke her family with the cry, "War is coming; I heard the Duke of Rodenstein!" Her relatives laughed and told her she had been dreaming, but on the night of August 4 the German army invaded Belgium, plunging Eu-

rope into the First World War. A teacher and several other witnesses testified in writing that on August 5, between four and six in the afternoon, they heard a loud rustling noise and the clatter of invisible wagons in the sky above Nieder Kainsbach, one of several small towns in the valley.

As the Rodenstein tradition suggests, castles on the continent are at least as likely to be thought haunted as those in the British Isles. Nor must the castle be situated in such a gloomy site as the Odenwald forest. Sicily's Carini Castle, built on a rocky cliff on the lower slope of Mount Cesarea west of Palermo, looks out over the shining Mediterranean. It is said to be haunted by the spirit of a beautiful sixteenth-century baroness of Carini.

According to an account published in 1992 by the castle staff, the ghostly baroness was Laura Lanza, who in 1543, at the age of fourteen, was married to sixteen-year-old Vincenzo La Grua. She was whisked away from an enjoyable life at court in Palermo to isolated Castle Carini, a twelfth-century edifice built during the Norman occupation of the island. As in the story of the German Rodenstein family, Laura's young husband frequently left her alone, and the marriage was not a happy one. Many years passed, and the baroness eventu-

ally fell in love with Ludovico Vernagallo, the dashing heir to nearby estates at Montelepre.

When Laura had been married twenty years, the gossiping of a local friar carried tales of her infidelity to her husband, Vincenzo La Grua. He enlisted the aid of Laura's ruthless father, Don Cesare, who viewed any unfaithfulness on his daughter's part as a stain on his honor as well as her husband's. Together they rode to La Grua's castle bent on vengeance. It was Don Cesare who is said to have flung open the door to his daughter's rooms and—according to some accounts—caught the couple flagrante delicto. Others insist that no physical infidelity ever took place. In any case, Don Cesare reportedly plunged his sword into Laura's heart. Then he called on his son-in-law to dispatch Laura's lover. The double murder, if such it indeed was, is recorded with an austere entry in the death registry in the main church of Carini: "On 4 December 1563 the Signora Laura La Grua died." And then: "Ludovico Vernagallo died."

No tears were wasted on the dissolute Vernagallo, but the whole of Sicily is said to have wept at the death of the beautiful Laura, although her innocence or guilt remains a matter of debate. Popular tradition has it that Laura's ghost still haunts the castle, perhaps looking for her father. She is

dressed in elegant clothes of the period—wide skirts of heavy silk, a tight bodice, a fringed shawl, and a small hat held by a long pin. Another tradition has it that the ghost of her father also appears; having learned too late of her innocence, he now repents his murderous act.

Much less is known about another ghost—considerably less romantic than the lovely Laura—which reportedly haunted a small family farmhouse near the town of Schweizer-Reneke in South Africa's western Transvaal Province early in the twentieth century. Like the spirits thought to have besieged Ireland's Gill Hall and the Caledonia Mills farm in Nova Scotia, the presence seemed to fit the standard model of a poltergeist, persistent and actively destructive. Unlike most poltergeists, however, the phantom, known as "Old Griet," was reportedly seen several times. Witnesses described it as having a man's shape, although the ghost was given a woman's name because of speculation that an unhappy female worker might be at the root of the matter. According to a certain Mr. K., who owned the farm and who claimed to have witnessed Old Griet's eerie appearances, the phantom "walked bent forward, taking long strides, and had big feet. It wore a large broad-brimmed hat and its clothes were in rags."

Old Griet's hauntings are said to have begun one night when Mr. K.'s brother-in-law and sister were awakened by something pulling at their toes. Some time after that, as reported by Mr. K., the ash bucket floated out of the kitchen, "as if carried by some invisible person," moved through the house, out the front door, around to the back of the house, and up to the ash heap. "Quite a number of us followed the bucket," according to Mr. K. "The ash was emptied on to the heap and the bucket thrown aside. I picked it up myself and carried it indoors."

One night, after Mr. K. and a teacher who lodged with them had hidden some sticks under the mattress in hopes of catching and beating the ghost, Old Griet reportedly attacked the teacher instead, dealing him a blow to the chin with one of the sticks that left a permanent scar. On another bright, moonlit night, Old Griet was supposedly seen standing wrapped in a wool blanket on the corner of the corral. Mr. K.'s father fired his rifle at the eerie specter and it fell backward, but when the family ran over to look, the phantom reappeared, unharmed, on another corner.

As with the poltergeist that allegedly bedeviled the MacDonalds on their farm in Nova Scotia, Old Griet's fate has never been recorded. In 1912, Mr. K.'s family sold the place and moved away.

Vague and unexplained in their origins, poltergeists like Old Griet remain a frustrating mystery to many psychic investigators. But poltergeists are hardly the only haunting agents to lack a clearly defined personal history. In Asia, many ghosts are essentially generic; China's "hungry ghosts," for example, are said to be the angry spirits of all the dead who are insufficiently honored by the living.

Other Asian ghost stories, although based on real events, have assumed the status of legend—none more so than the tale of a Japanese woman known simply as Oiwa, who died more than four centuries ago. A shrine marks Oiwa's birthplace in the Yotsuya section of Tokyo, and in another district of the city called Sugamo, her tomb has a place of honor in a temple graveyard. In the centuries since her death Oiwa has been honored in the art and legends of Japan as one of the best-known—and most vindictive—ghosts in a country whose culture includes a veritable host of phantoms.

What is known of the real Oiwa is quickly told, although the precise details may vary. She was born around 1600, the only child of a low-ranking samurai; when she was a girl, she lost an eye to measles. In her early thirties, despite her disfigurement, she found a husband, named Iemon, who, sadly, proved to be a thoroughly bad householder. In short order, he forced Oiwa to disgrace herself by becoming a servant maid in someone else's house. That made room at home for his own mistress and her baby—a child fathered not by him but by a government official.

When Oiwa realized the scope of Iemon's betrayal, she went mad and shortly afterward died. But almost immediately her ghost returned to wreak terrible vengeance. Iemon himself became insane and died—one version of the story says he drowned himself in a river to escape her hauntings—and his mistress and a reported eighteen members of their families also died within a few years.

Oiwa's ghost has since been celebrated in art, where she is portrayed as a harridan with a horribly bulging eye. In a popular Kabuki play, written in 1825, she becomes a beautiful girl disfigured by Iemon's poisons. More recently she has been featured in several movies. To this day, Oiwa is considered a potent spirit not to be taken lightly. Prospective producers of films about her reportedly begin their projects by visiting her well-tended grave, where they politely ask Oiwa's spirit not to harm their enterprises.

Far from Oiwa's grave amid bustling Tokyo, a little-known ghost with a taste for the more rural life after death reportedly frequents a clearing in the bush of Australia's vast central desert about a hundred miles from the town of Alice Springs. Perhaps because its haunt is so remote and sparsely settled, alleged sightings of the Ghost of the Outback, as some have dubbed it, are rare, and no stories of particular occurrences involving it have reached the world at large. But in May 1956, a visitor from Adelaide, the Reverend R. S. Blance, is reported to have taken a photograph of the phantom. The image, showing a short, dark-featured figure, lent support to the theory that the clearing's ghost may be that of an Aborigine; tradition has it that as late as the nineteenth century the place was used by the indigenous Arunta people for secret—and sometimes fatal—initiation rites. Some have speculated that the supposed shade is the spirit of a tribesman who died in one of the rituals.

Alone in the bush, the anonymous phantom seems to bear final witness to the relationship long posited between supposed ghosts and the particular places they are said to haunt. Humans may stumble upon ghosts, attempt to exorcise or release them, photograph or tape-record their ghostly appearances, and even—in the case of poltergeists—come to blows with them. But in the final analysis, the living appear no more than irrelevant bystanders to a phenomenon upon which they themselves have little effect. It is the lonely houses, ancient castles, and other haunted places of the world that engage the attention of any real phantoms—the places, not the people, that they knew in life which seem to control their destiny forever in death.

The tradition that the phantom duke of Rodenstein and his men thunder through German skies as wars begin and end probably inspired their appearance on the 10-pfennig scrip above, used instead of coin to conserve metal during World War I. Rodenstein Castle (left) is now an overgrown ruin, having been uninhabited since 1640, six years after the duke's wife, Marie von Hochberg (below), died uttering a curse on her husband. Twentieth-century reports say houses and barns tremble and animals become jumpy when the duke's noisy horde passes overhead.

Mysteries of the Skies

On August 27, 1956, a Royal Canadian Air Force pilot flying over the Rocky Mountains of Alberta saw an immense, brilliant disk of light hovering within a thunderhead. Quickly reaching for a camera, he snapped a picture of the strange luminescence *(right)*. Although the negative was scratched, as can be seen here, physicist Bruce Maccabee analyzed the pilot's photo and declared that the circle of light at right-center defies scientific explanation: It is an unidentified flying object—a UFO.

The pilot's experience was just one of thousands of strange events that have been witnessed in the sky, making the atmosphere fully as rich in mystery as earth's lands and waters. In fact, as the map that follows reveals, UFO sightings have been reported over every continent and every ocean. Many wondrous aerial phenomena were recorded long before the sky became a familiar milieu for human travel. An ancient Chinese tale describes strange winged chariots. A Sanskrit text tells of magical flying machines. The armies of Alexander the Great supposedly experienced threats from two airborne objects. A ninth-century French cleric wrote of a complaint by peasants that "aerial sailors" were destroying their crops. Even the Bible makes reference to mysterious aircraft, such as the wheel-within-a-wheel vehicles of the prophet Ezekiel's vision.

Since the birth of the air age, the skies have posed more unanswered questions than ever before. During World War II, "foo fighters"—unexplained lights—harried both Allied and Axis pilots. And after the UFO era dawned with the alleged sighting of a "flying saucer" by an Idaho man in 1947, the incidence of reports skyrocketed. Some of the most significant are summarized on these pages.

1

As the U.S.S. Supply was crossing the North Pacific in 1904, sailors reported being tracked by a formation of three "remarkable meteors."

2

Russian artist and explorer Nikolay Roerich and his companions on a 1926 Himalayan trek claimed they saw a "big and shiny" object "moving at great speed" in the sky.

3

While flying over Washington State in 1947, Idaho pilot Kenneth Arnold mistook a formation of bright objects for jets—until he saw they had no tails.

4

After a Roswell, New Mexico, couple saw "two inverted saucers" in the sky in 1947, debris was found nearby that some said was from crashed UFOs.

5

The crew of an East African Airways plane flying over Mount Kilimanjaro in 1951 caught sight of "a metallic, bullet-shaped object over 200 feet long."

6

On a summer night in 1952, seven unknown objects appeared on a radar scope at the air-traffic-control center of National Airport in Washington, D.C.

7

During the month of September 1952, a wave of UFO sightings swept northern Europe. Many NATO military personnel reported strangely maneuvering spheres, triangles, and disks.

8

Crew members and passengers on a British Overseas Airways plane flying 150 miles south of Labrador in 1954 reported seeing an airborne "blob" surrounded by six smaller objects.

9

In 1957, a young Brazilian farmer reported he had been taken aboard an alien craft, where a female extraterrestrial allegedly seduced him in hopes of conceiving a hybrid baby.

10

During a string of purported UFO sightings in New Guinea in 1959, witnesses claimed they waved to aliens aboard a low-flying spaceship—and that the aliens returned the gesture.

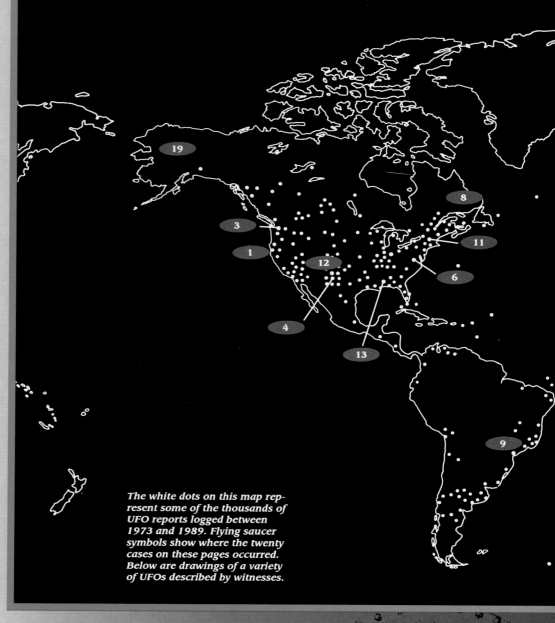

The white dots on this map represent some of the thousands of UFO reports logged between 1973 and 1989. Flying saucer symbols show where the twenty cases on these pages occurred. Below are drawings of a variety of UFOs described by witnesses.

11
A New Hampshire couple, Betty and Barney Hill, said that in 1961 they were abducted from their car by aliens piloting a tilting, luminous disk.

12
In 1964, a New Mexico police officer reported finding an egg-shaped craft in a gully. Two white-clad humanoids allegedly emerged and stood by the craft.

13
Two Pascagoula, Mississippi, fishermen claimed that in October 1973 they were abducted by aliens and subjected to medical examinations inside a UFO.

14
In 1976, two Iranian Air Force jets inspecting a strange craft over Tehran reportedly lost crucial functions—one as it neared the UFO, the other when chased by a glowing device the UFO launched.

15
Flying over Australia's Bass Strait, a young civilian pilot and his plane vanished in 1978 moments after he radioed to ground control that a strange aircraft was hovering over him.

16
A domed UFO with a flashing red light allegedly landed in a Kuwaiti oil field in 1978. No physical evidence was found, but additional sightings were reported for several months.

17
On December 27, 1980, U.S. airmen stationed in Woodbridge, England, reportedly found a landed UFO and, according to rumors, its crew—three-foot-tall aliens.

18
A UFO is said to have landed in Trans-en-Provence, France, in 1981, leaving circular impressions in the ground and apparently altering the genetic make-up of grasses it had touched.

19
Flying over Alaska in 1986, a Japan Air Lines cargo plane reportedly encountered three UFOs. One came so close that the pilot felt the need to request a course change to evade it.

20
An absurd 1989 Soviet report of a UFO landing in Voronezh may have been a smoke screen to mask government alarm over a real alien encounter.

CHAPTER 2

Hidden Creatures

egularly drenched in rain yet renowned for its equally frequent sunshine, southern Florida is a land of immense contrasts, none greater than between the cosmopolitan city of Miami and the vast Everglades swamp that begins only ten miles to its west. A combination of sawgrass marsh and water-logged cypress forest, the Everglades once sheltered runaway slaves and Seminole Indians who took refuge from white pursuers in the forbidding wilderness. Today the Seminole live on a few reservations in and around the Everglades. Most of the swamp is reserved for such indigenous wildlife as the Everglades mink, the mangrove fox squirrel, and the Florida panther—and, according to rumor and repeated sightings, a mysterious humanlike beast commonly referred to as the Florida Skunk Ape.

Like the Abominable Snowman, or Yeti, that is reputed to roam the Himalayas, or the so-called Bigfoot of the American Northwest, the Skunk Ape is described as a huge, hairy biped more than seven feet tall. Its name is a reference to the creature's peculiarly fetid odor, which is perhaps to be expected in a hairy animal that lives in a swamp. Little known before the twentieth century, the Skunk Ape was reportedly seen more often after the Florida construction boom of the 1920s, with a great upsurge of sightings during the 1960s and 1970s. These alleged sightings, some inside the swamp and others near the garbage dumps, chicken coops, and rabbit hutches of southern Florida towns, suggest to some researchers that the Skunk Ape has been forced from its secluded habitat by encroaching human activity. Others, including most zoologists and other scientists, dismiss the entire matter as a local myth.

Up until 1970, no one was more skeptical of the Skunk Ape legend than engineer and amateur archaeologist H. C. "Buz" Osborn. Osborn and four companions said they found reason to change that opinion while examining a Native American burial mound in southern Florida. Asleep in their tents not far from the mound on a cool February night, the five enthusiasts reportedly awakened at three in the morning to find an eight-foot-tall humanoid standing outside their tent. Covered in light-colored hair, the unwelcome visitor smelled "awful," in the words of one witness, but did no harm and soon disappeared into the darkness. In the morning, the group found five-toed footprints that measured seventeen and a half inches long and eleven inches wide at the toes. Osborn later commented that he had never believed in Skunk Apes, but that the early morning visit "made a believer out of me."

Skunk Apes may be nocturnal in their habits, for another well-known sighting came just after midnight on January 9, 1974, when Richard Lee Smith of Hollywood, Florida, ran his car into a large animal on State Road 27. Smith told the *Miami Herald* he believed his unintended victim was "a gorilla, a strange creature of some sort," and described it as "huge, seven or eight feet tall, dark-colored and humanlike." He said that after the accident it limped away into the Everglades. Police agreed that motorist Smith had struck "something" with his car but commented that "it was dark and at night and he doesn't know what he hit."

During the 1970s, researcher Ramona Hibner combined information from dozens of purported Florida sightings to develop a profile of the typical Skunk Ape. As befits a swamp creature, the ape never goes far from water, Hibner found. It apparently feeds on small animals and such plant delicacies as cactus pulp, water lily bulbs, and oranges. Hibner, who claims to have seen the Skunk Ape more than once, recalls that one such creature had "an earthy smell, not at all unpleasant." Despite these

and other sightings, the Skunk Ape has so far avoided giving any definitive proof of its existence, a distinction it may unhappily retain as the shrinking Florida wetlands reduce the creature's supposed habitat, perhaps beyond the limits of livability.

The Everglades swamp is only one of the world's many out-of-the-way places said to conceal creatures unrecognized by modern science. Over the centuries, puzzling animals have been reported by thousands of independent witnesses around the world. Remote wilderness areas ranging from the Everglades to the Himalayas are said to hold human-like beasts; large cold-water lakes from Lake Champlain to Siberia have been linked to huge aquatic animals with barrel chests and long necks. And areas in both South America and Africa are said to hide a number of large, as-yet-unrecognized animal species, many of them with a taste for human flesh.

Nor are more settled regions immune from occasional incursions by unknown creatures. As recently as the 1980s, a mysterious animal slaughtered pets in the town of Truro in Massachusetts's Cape Cod, and only a few years earlier a flying man-beast frightened a number of young witnesses on England's Cornish coast. Unlike the Skunk Ape and other denizens of remote areas, strange animals in populated areas are usually reported during a brief period and then never seen again—suggesting that these particular creatures, if indeed they exist, may be inadvertent visitors from a more sheltered wilderness area.

Despite frequent sightings, blurry photographs, and much-interpreted footprints, however, the absence of clear scientific proof has kept the existence of many supposed species an open question. To promote further study of the matter, some scientifically oriented researchers have established a field of study known as cryptozoology, literally the science of secret or hidden animals. Cryptozoologists base

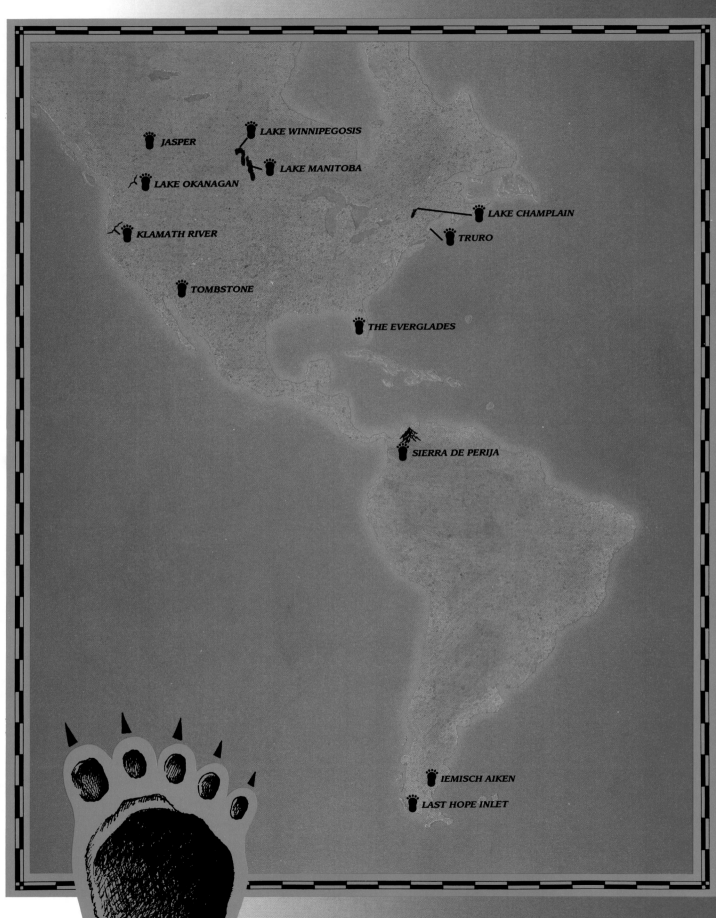

JASPER

LAKE WINNIPEGOSIS

LAKE MANITOBA

LAKE OKANAGAN

LAKE CHAMPLAIN

KLAMATH RIVER

TRURO

TOMBSTONE

THE EVERGLADES

SIERRA DE PERIJA

IEMISCH AIKEN

LAST HOPE INLET

their work on the notion that relatively unexplored areas of the world may very well contain unknown zoological surprises, perhaps even large, "monstrous" animals.

As proof, they point to the twentieth-century discovery of such sizable animals as the pygmy hippopotamus and the coelacanth, a five-foot-long fish with bulging blue eyes and padded, leglike fins previously believed to have been extinct for more than 60 million years. If the coelacanth survived unobserved to the modern era, say the cryptozoologists, it is not too far-fetched to assume that some of the world's other seemingly legendary monsters may also exist, concealed in habitats that hide as well as support life.

In the Americas, a common clue to the existence of such creatures lies in folk traditions among the indigenous peoples of the New World. Early European colonists often dismissed tales of apparent American monsters as unbelievable—a conclusion that in several cases may have been arrived at too hastily. Even today, a number of these supposedly mythical creatures have

Mask of a horned monster, Venezuela

been sighted roaming the continents of North and South America, frightening newcomers and old inhabitants alike.

Among the most often reported are freshwater lake monsters in the vast interconnecting North American systems of cold-water lakes and rivers. The most famous of these elusive creatures is said to reside in Lake Okanagan, a glacier-formed stretch of water located in the western Canadian province of British Columbia. Seventy-nine miles long, two miles wide, and 800 feet deep, the lake was known to local Salish Indians as N'ha-a-itk, a name variously translated as "water god," "lake demon," and "snake of the water," and a seemingly likely reference to ancient knowledge of the Okanagan creature.

Although sightings of the beast have been reported for centuries, it was only in the 1920s that such glimpses began to be documented with any regularity. One of the best-known incidents took place on the morning of July 19, 1926, when John and Isabella Logie and their two grandchildren, thirteen-year-old Catherine and eleven-year-old Robert, were driving along the western shore of the lake on a calm summer day.

STRANGE BEASTS OF THE AMERICAS

THE EVERGLADES
The hairy, humanoid Skunk Ape that supposedly prowls this Florida swamp has been reported since the 1920s. Witnesses say Skunk Apes range in height from five to eight feet and weigh hundreds of pounds.

IEMISCH AIKEN
The Iemisch, a ferocious beast said to lurk in south Argentine waters, reportedly surfaced from Argentina's Rio Santa Cruz near this site, which is named "harbor of the Iemisch" in a local Indian language.

JASPER
In 1811, tracks found in the snow outside this town in Alberta were linked to the giant man-beast known in Canada as the Sasquatch. Sightings of the elusive creature are still reported in western Canada.

KLAMATH RIVER
A film shot in 1967 near this river appears to depict a shaggy humanoid known in the Pacific Northwest as Bigfoot. Although controversial, the movie remains the best evidence of the creature's existence.

LAKE CHAMPLAIN
Allegedly dwelling in this New England lake is a serpentine monster called Champ. Reported sightings of the beast and its ancestors began in the early seventeenth century and continued into the twentieth.

LAKE MANITOBA
Dubbed Manipogo, the huge humped creature said to live in this Canadian lake has been reported seen so often that in 1957 the Canadian government authorized a search for it. The hunt turned up nothing.

LAKE OKANAGAN
In this lake in British Columbia supposedly lurks the long-necked, small-headed monster known as Ogopogo. Tradition has it that Indians used to appease the creature with offerings of live animals.

LAKE WINNIPEGOSIS
Winnipogo, a large beast said to dwell in this Manitoba lake, is one of the few Canadian lake monsters linked to physical evidence: a bone shaped like a giant vertebra that was discovered here in the 1930s.

LAST HOPE INLET
A landowner found a strange hide near this Chilean fjord in the 1890s. The find gave support to tales of the Su monster, described in a sixteenth-century account as "very dreadful and obnoxious."

TOMBSTONE
A persistent story claims that a giant flying creature was shot dead outside this Arizona city in 1886. Some believe the animal may have been the enormous Thunderbird described in Native American legend.

TRURO
Pet slayings that plagued this Cape Cod town in 1981 were attributed to a mysterious animal visitor. One theory held that the Beast of Truro was a mountain lion, officially considered extinct in Massachusetts.

SIERRA DE PERIJA
In these mountains on the Colombia-Venezuela border, an expedition led by a Swiss geologist in the 1920s reportedly killed a hitherto unknown creature—upright, apelike, and more than five feet tall.

Annotated with precise lengths, the sketch at left is based on a cast taken from a supposed Florida Skunk Ape footprint in 1971. Skunk Ape feet may be even wider than those of the similar Bigfoot, for good reason: Broad feet would be well-suited to the spongy soil of the Great Cypress Swamp (above).

Suddenly, according to their later recollections, the family observed "undulations" in the water that seemed to be caused by "a rather strange looking animal," about twenty feet long, with a head like an earless bulldog's. Its face was said to resemble a sheep's with a pointed nose. The Logies said they paced the creature at about thirty miles an hour for several miles.

A few months later, the composer of a Canadian parody of an English song made reference to Lake Okanagan's alleged monster under the nickname Ogopogo. Although meaningless, the name stuck, and sightings of Ogopogo continued year after year. In 1967, for example, fifteen employees of a local cannery came out to join Mr. and Mrs. John Durrant of British Columbia in a brief observation of a strange, humped serpentine animal that the Durrants had glimpsed as it rose above the lake's surface just off the shore at Natamata, a small town at the southern tip of Lake Okanagan. "It had a head like a bucket and was spouting water," reported Mrs. Durrant. "We've seen whales and seals and things, but it was nothing like that. This was something different."

For all the sightings at Lake Okanagan, however, Ogopogo is relatively camera-shy; the few photographs of the beast show only disturbances in the water. A better image exists of Manipogo, a lake monster named after Ogopogo. Manipogo supposedly dwells in Lake Manitoba, a 125-mile-long, tree-lined body of water in Canada's Manitoba province, some 750 miles east of Lake Okanagan. The photo was taken on August 12, 1962, by two Canadian fishermen and an American. Unlike the Ogopogo snapshots, it shows a large, snakelike creature, but it remains too indistinct to be a conclusive indication of Manipogo's existence.

An equally intriguing piece of evidence is associated with another Manitoba lake, Winnipegosis, where Manitoba resident Oscar Frederickson supposedly found an unusual bone, possibly that of a lake monster, in the 1930s. Since then, a fire has destroyed the bone, although a wooden model of the original still exists. It resembles a very large spinal vertebra, but without the original bone the model cannot be considered final proof of a local lake monster.

Far to the east of Lake Manitoba, 109-mile-long Lake Champlain divides New York and Vermont before it stretches into Quebec. Although small compared to the neighboring Great Lakes, Champlain is said to hold one of the most commonly sighted North American lake monsters. Affectionately called Champ by local residents, the beast—or its ancestors—may have been spotted in 1609 by Samuel de Champlain, the French explorer after whom the lake is named, when he reportedly glimpsed a serpentlike creature that was about twenty feet long, with a body shaped like a barrel and a head like a horse's. Local Iroquois legend also describes a ''Great Horned Serpent,'' which has been interpreted as an even earlier reference to Champ.

Alleged sightings of Champ, often clustered near Bulwagga Bay at the lake's southern end, increased significantly during the nineteenth century and have continued unabated, with at least 200 instances on record. By 1981, interest in Champ grew to such proportions that a scientific conference on the possible existence of the monster was held in Port Henry, New York, not far from Bulwagga Bay. Stymied by a lack of absolute proof of the monster's existence, the scientists reached no definitive conclusions.

Many cryptozoologists, although not absolutely sure Champ exists, are confident that cold-water lake monsters do. Sighted in cold climates around the world in deep freshwater lakes, these creatures have such a remarkable consistency of appearance, behavior, and habitat that ''one could hardly wish for better circumstantial evidence of their existence,'' wrote French cryptozoologist Bernard Heuvelmans, a leading authority in the field, in 1986. Like Champ, Ogopogo, and the other Canadian curiosities, most of the world's cold-water lake monsters are reported to have long, dark bodies, about twenty to forty feet in length, and small but elongated heads, sometimes with ears or tiny protruding horns.

From this general description, cryptozoologists theorize that the monsters could be either ancient marine reptiles known as plesiosaurs or ancient primitive whales known as zeuglodons. Both animals were thought to have become extinct millions of years ago. Until more substantial evidence comes to light, however, the identity of Canada's lake monsters will remain as murky as the deep waters in which they pass much of their days.

Heavily populated Cape Cod is a far cry from the Canadian lakes, but an anomalous beast nevertheless turned up on that curving Massachusetts peninsula in September 1981. That fall, as later reported in the *New York Times,* the people of the small town of Truro near the tip of the cape began to report the inexplicable maiming and killing of cats and other domestic animals.

At first, people attributed the troubling incidents to packs of wild dogs, which are known to kill deer. Then several residents sighted a large, catlike animal lurking about the town. One couple, William and Marsha Mendeiros, told the *Times* that they came within fifty feet of the creature

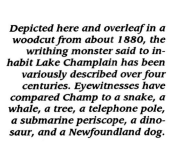

Depicted here and overleaf in a woodcut from about 1880, the writhing monster said to inhabit Lake Champlain has been variously described over four centuries. Eyewitnesses have compared Champ to a snake, a whale, a tree, a telephone pole, a submarine periscope, a dinosaur, and a Newfoundland dog.

while walking on the beach. "It had a very definite long ropelike tail like the letter J," they reported, which "hit the ground and went up. We figured it was about as tall as up to our knees and weighed sixty to eighty pounds." Afraid the animal might attack, William stooped to pick up a stick, but the creature quietly slipped into the nearby woods and disappeared among the trees.

The Mendeiroses are among those who believe that the Beast of Truro, as it has become known, may have been an Eastern mountain lion, an animal generally thought to be extinct, but which may have somehow survived in the undeveloped national seashore area near Truro. But at least one nearby resident, a former zoo employee, believes instead that the beast may have been simply an escaped pet ocelot, lynx, or other large wild cat. The animal has not been seen since January 1982, however, so no one may ever know for sure.

A far more persistent American mystery is that of a gigantic flying creature known as the Thunderbird, said to roam the dry, rugged mountains of the southwestern United States. Described in many Native American traditions, the Thunderbird is believed by some scholars to be a semi-legendary creature based on the exploits of either the eagle or the California condor, one of the world's largest—and rarest—birds. Others believe that the real Thunderbird is an unknown flying animal that may have existed as recently as the last century or may even be alive today.

One tantalizing clue lies in an alleged incident dating to 1886, when several ranchers living near Tombstone, Arizona, reportedly shot and killed an enormous bird whose wingspan exceeded thirty feet, more than four times the wingspan of the California condor. After nailing their trophy with its wings spread wide to the side of a barn, the ranchers supposedly took a photograph of it with six men posed in front of the bird, their arms outstretched. Unfortunately, the photograph, if it ever existed, has disappeared. Searches of the files of the *Tombstone Epitaph,* where it was said to have been published, come up empty.

Cryptozoologists point out that the specimen described in 1886 sounds remarkably like one of the prehistoric flying reptiles known as teratorns, which once ruled the skies over Nevada and California. Could the bird shot down in 1886 have been a living teratorn, one that somehow survived until modern times? Skeptics ridicule the idea, but rumored Thunderbird sightings persist.

The Thunderbird, if it is a living teratorn, may not be the only supposedly prehistoric creature still alive and well in the Americas. At the southern tip of South America, more than 5,000 miles from the land of the Thunderbird, the Tehuelche Indians of Argentina have long told of a four-legged, coarse-haired beast as big as an ox that allegedly inhabits the Patagonian pampas, the sweeping grass-covered plains east of the Andes. Sleeping all day in burrows that it digs with its enormous claws, the animal is said to roam the pampas at night. The Teheulche call the creature Su or Succarath, which means "cloak of skin," and their ancestors supposedly hunted it for its thick, armorlike hide. By some accounts, the Su is quite savage, capable of killing an entire herd of horses or, according to one story, a whole Tehuelche family.

Nineteenth-century paleontologists believed that tales of the Su might result from distorted memories of the giant ground sloth, an animal that thrived in South America until about 10,000 years ago when, for unknown reasons, it became extinct. But a discovery during the 1890s made people wonder if the giant ground sloth, or something resem-

Chile's serene Last Hope Inlet (opposite, top) lies near the cave in which a bone-studded hide was discovered in 1895, lending credence to local belief in the so-called Su monster. Supposedly, the Su carries its young on its back, as shown in a fanciful sketch of the Su (opposite, bottom left) published in 1558 by French priest André Thévet. His and other accounts have led some to speculate that the Su was a surviving example of the prehistoric ground sloth known as the mylodon (opposite, bottom right), thought by most scientists to be extinct.

bling it, might still inhabit remote regions of Patagonia.

In 1895 a German immigrant farmer known locally as Captain Eberhardt found an unusual piece of hide in a cave on his property in southern Argentina. Embedded with small bony nodules—an odd feature also common to the skins of certain prehistoric ground sloths—the hide was so tough it could be cut only with an ax or a saw. It appeared to be fresh and had been found rolled up, as if by human hands. Pieces of the hide were sent to experts in South America and in Europe. Given the resources of their era, the researchers had no way of determining the age of the strange skin, although they concluded that it seemed to be from a large sloth—much larger than any sloth known to be still living in South America. Similar pieces of hide have also been found in other South American caves.

Another animal common in Tehuelche lore is the savage Iemisch or Water-tiger, which is said to attack horses and cattle as they swim across rivers. Like the Su, the Iemisch was thought by European scientists to be either mythical or long extinct—until a turn-of-the-century report seemed to suggest otherwise.

In 1900, a French traveler named André Tournouër said he saw an Iemisch (or *hymche* as he called it) during a fossil-collecting expedition to southern Argentina for the Paris Museum. "Lying in wait one evening on the bank of a river in the interior, beside which I had pitched my camp, I saw emerge in the middle of the stream the head of an animal the size of a large puma," he wrote in a letter to his former teacher Albert Gaudry. Gaudry later read the letter to the Académie des Sciences in Paris. "I fired, the animal

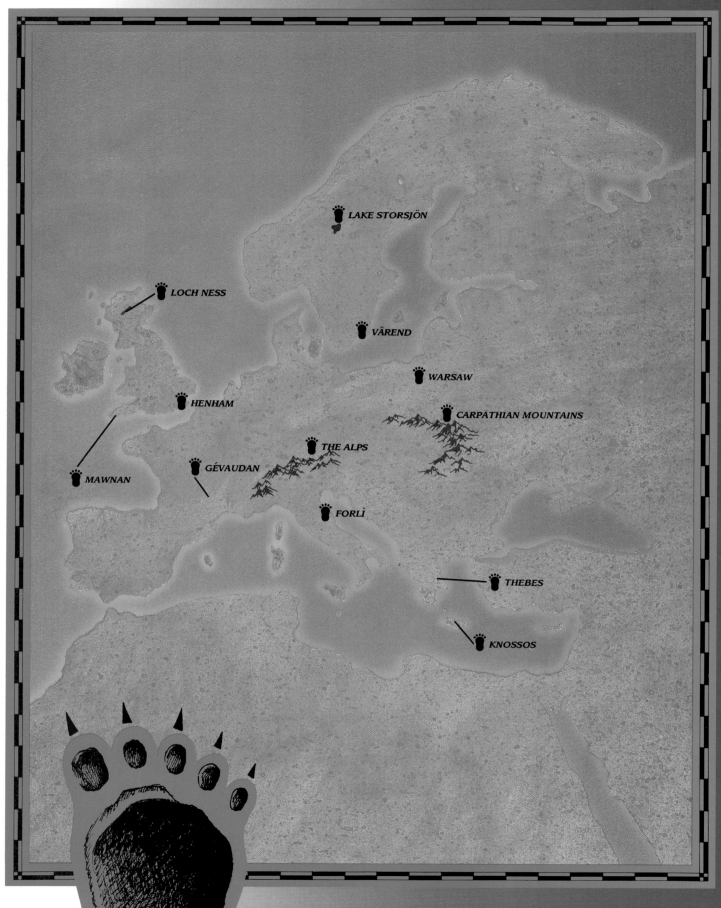

LAKE STORSJÖN

LOCH NESS

VÄREND

WARSAW

HENHAM

CARPATHIAN MOUNTAINS

THE ALPS

MAWNAN

GÉVAUDAN

FORLÌ

THEBES

KNOSSOS

dived and did not reappear. As far as I could see in the dusk, its round head had dark brown fur, its eyes were encircled with light yellow hair, stretching in a thin line to the earhole. There was no external ear. I described it to the Indian who acted as my guide; he seemed very frightened and assured me I had seen the mysterious *hymche.*"

Despite Tournouër's alarming report, anthropologists familiar with the Tehuelche culture doubt the existence of the Iemisch, suggesting instead that the Tehuelche may have transferred the ferocious characteristics of the jaguar, which once used to live as far south as Patagonia and is fearless of water, to the Patagonian river otter, a peaceful aquatic mammal. Cryptozoologists, however, are intrigued by reports of the Iemisch. If it exists, they say, the Iemisch may be some unknown variety of giant otter or even an extant saber-toothed tiger. To date, several twentieth-century expeditions into Patagonia in search of the elusive animal have come back empty-handed.

And so the case stands for most of the mysterious creatures of the Americas, fabled or actual residents of a series of lands that stretch from the shores of the Arctic

Image of a crowing dragon, seventeenth century

Ocean to the southern Strait of Magellan. Tantalizing partial evidence, innumerable sightings, and plausible theories of their origins have failed to date to lure the Iemisch, the Thunderbird, or any Canadian lake monsters out of hiding into the full light of acknowledged zoological fact.

Like their counterparts in the Americas, a number of European rivers, lakes, mountains, and forests are said to be inhabited by mysterious and often monstrous creatures, although the continent's more settled terrain produces subtly different enigmas. What remote areas remain, however, offer their own mysteries. Perhaps none is better known than the long-necked lake serpent said to live in Scotland's Loch Ness, the largest freshwater lake in the British Isles. But Nessie, highly reminiscent of Canadian lake monsters, is not unique even in Europe. Just about 750 miles northeast of Loch Ness in mountainous central Sweden, generations of local residents and visitors have reported their sightings of what has been called the second most often seen lake monster in the world, the Storsjöodjuret, or Great Lake Monster of Lake Storsjön.

The deepest of Sweden's 90,000 lakes, Lake Storsjön lies 280 miles north-northwest of Stock-

EUROPE'S RUMORED MONSTERS

THE ALPS
For more than a century, a two-footed lizard known as the Tatzelwurm has been reported in the Alps. Never recognized by science, the long-tailed biped was supposedly seen as recently as 1929.

CARPATHIAN MOUNTAINS
Throughout the Middle Ages—and as late as 1784—reports of hairy humanoids called Wild Men or Wudewása abounded in this Eastern European mountain range.

FORLÌ
In 1970 a huge reptile resembling a dragon, with large paws and fiery breath, reportedly chased a farm worker near this town in Italy. Three other witnesses also claimed they saw the fifteen-foot-long beast.

GÉVAUDAN
A special Catholic mass and a hail of silver bullets reportedly put an end to a mysterious wolflike beast blamed for slaughtering children in this part of south-central France from 1764 to 1767.

HENHAM
Witnesses near this Essex village could not catch what they described as a dragon, eight feet long, sighted in 1669. The sharp-toothed creature supposedly scrambled away into a forest after evading pursuers.

KNOSSOS
In ancient times a beast called the Minotaur was said to roam a mazelike complex in this Cretan city's royal palace. Built like a man but with a bull's head, the creature supposedly feasted on sacrificial maidens.

LAKE STORSJÖN
Sweden's deepest lake purportedly holds the Storsjöodjuret, a large, coiled monster reported there since the 1770s. Local law protects the supposed lake dweller from harm.

LOCH NESS
Allegedly sighted some 3,000 times since 1880, the Loch Ness monster has long drawn investigators to this Scottish lake. But sonar, underwater cameras, and minisubmarines have produced no monster.

MAWNAN
On three occasions in 1976, visitors to a church in this coastal Cornish town claimed they saw a large, manlike creature with wings and an owl's head flying above nearby trees.

THEBES
The Sphinx, a bizarre beast with a lion's body, an eagle's wings, and a woman's head, is said to have guarded the road to this ancient Greek city, killing those who did not answer her questions correctly.

VÄREND
Accounts from nineteenth-century Scandinavia claim that a poison-spitting, twenty-foot-long black snake known as a Lindorm roamed the countryside near this Swedish town.

WARSAW
In 1587, frightened citizens in the Polish capital city organized one of the last hunts for a Basilisk, a snake with a rooster's head and a deadly gaze. They found and killed a small serpent in a cellar.

53

Above, modern reenactors on the shores of Sweden's Lake Storsjön bait a lake-monster trap with a dead pig. Constructed in the 1890s, the device never caught its intended prey—and a local legend suggests why. Tradition says Storsjön's supposed monster cannot leave its watery home until someone deciphers the runes on the ancient stone at right, found on an island in the lake.

holm near the mountain town of Östersund. Much like other cold-water lake monsters, the Storsjön beast is said to have a long, humped body, a round head, short stumpy legs or feet, and little ears that look like tiny sails and can be laid back tight along the neck.

During the nineteenth century, there were frequent local reports of the monster. In 1820 a frightened farmer claimed that the creature had followed his boat for some time at the south end of the lake. When a railway was built to the town in the 1880s, news of Lake Storsjön's monster spread beyond Östersund. By 1894, reported sightings of the Storsjöodjuret had become so numerous that a wealthy widow in Östersund hired an experienced Norwegian whaler to land the elusive creature. King Oscar II, then the ruler of Sweden, is said to have contributed some money to

the venture, which ended a year later in failure when the funding ran out.

Reports of the Storsjöodjuret have continued throughout the twentieth century. In July 1976, for example, the Swedish newspaper *Expressen* described a close encounter experienced by Rolf Larsson and Irene Magnusson, who had been fishing on Lake Storsjön in a motorboat. Some waves rocked the boat, Larson said, and "we saw something that moved under the surface. Then it came up to the surface, not with a splash but with smooth waves."

Larsson said the creature, which looked to him like an upside-down boat, swam around his own craft, stunning him into immobility and terrifying his companion. At last, said Larsson, "Irene, who had been quiet all the time, shouted that I should immediately return to land. She was as pale as a corpse." But when the couple turned toward shore, the animal followed, Larsson recalled. "We were doing perhaps 10 knots, but the creature kept up with us. We returned to land, and we could see the wake of the creature for 5 or 6 minutes."

The Storsjön monster has purportedly been observed in all seasons, even in winter. Several witnesses have claimed they saw its smooth, round head break through Lake Storsjön's ice-capped surface. Usually, however, the creature is supposedly sighted during the warm summer months. Like Scotland's Nessie, the Storsjöodjuret attracts hundreds of tourists to its lake home each summer—a fact that leads some critics to say locals purposely promote belief in the monster.

If nineteenth-century reports are to be accepted, the sparsely settled Scandinavian countryside may offer unintended refuge to other mysterious creatures as well—in particular, the terrifying Lindorm, a giant dragonlike snake, ten to twenty feet long, with large teeth and a tough, scaly hide that was black everywhere except on its belly, which was yellow. The beast was said to recoil and hiss when alarmed, then spring forward to attack. Supposedly, the Lindorm then spat a poisonous liquid at those unfortunate people who had disturbed it.

Sightings of the Lindorm were said to occur near Värend, Sweden, and in remote Norwegian mountain lakes. Viewed as an unknown species of giant snake by nineteenth-century scholars, the Lindorm has more recently been used to bolster the idea that dragons really lived, as recently as the 1800s.

More evidence for dragons—in this case, those of the seventeenth century—comes from Great Britain. One of the more remarkable British dragon reports involved an eight-foot-long flying dragon seen by several groups of people in and about the village of Henham, England, in 1669. Witnesses said the winged creature had large, piercing eyes and two rows of sharp teeth. Whatever its identity, the animal soon disappeared for good into the nearby forest.

Three centuries after the dragon incident, another bizarre flying beast apparently took up residence in a British wood. During the 1970s, a huge, feathered bird-man was allegedly seen by many young girls in the quiet village of Mawnan in Cornwall on England's southwestern coast. The first sighting was reported on April 17, 1976, by June and Vicky Melling, two sisters aged twelve and nine years respectively, who were vacationing in Cornwall with their parents. They said they saw a strange winged creature hovering over the tower of Mawnan's church, which stands near the edge of a steep hill covered with trees.

Almost three months later, on the night of July 3, two fourteen-year-old girls camping in the woods near Mawnan Church saw the same mysterious bird-man. "It was like a big owl with pointed ears, as big as a man," one of the girls related. "The eyes were red and glowing. At first I thought it was someone dressed up, playing a joke, trying to scare us. I laughed at it, we both did, then it went up in the air and we both screamed. When it went up you could see its feet were like pincers."

The following morning two more vacationing English schoolgirls saw the flying creature. "It was in the trees standing like a full-grown man, but the legs bent backwards like a bird's," one of the girls, Jane Greenwood, later wrote in a letter to a local newspaper. "It saw us and quickly jumped up and rose straight up through the trees. My sister and I saw it very closely before it rose up. It has red

slanting eyes and a very large mouth. The feathers are silvery grey and so are his body and legs, the feet are like big black crab's claws.''

The beast was not reported again until June 1978, when a sixteen-year-old girl saw what she described as ''a monster like a devil flying up through the trees near old Mawnan Church.'' On August 2, three French girls also reported an encounter near the church with ''a great big furry bird with a gaping mouth and big round eyes.''

Some people believe that the Owlman of Mawnan, as the creature is sometimes called, was a hoax, perhaps devised by a young man to play on impressionable girls. Jane Greenwood even acknowledged that ''it could have been somebody playing a trick in very good costume and make-up.'' But then there is the puzzling matter of the creature's vertical flying ability. ''How could it rise up like that?'' asked Greenwood. The answer to that question may never be known, for the Owlman of Mawnan has not been observed flying in Cornwall—or anywhere else—since the French girls last saw it in 1978.

Across the English Channel, on the European continent, mysterious humanlike beasts have been sighted in or near forests for centuries. During the Middle Ages, many Europeans told of encounters with wild men, or Wudewása, which were invariably described as large, hairy humanoids. Accounts in the tomes of that era depicted the wild men as violent beasts, who emerged from the woods periodically to capture and eat people.

Some scholars trace the wild man stories back to ancient forest gods, while others suggest the wild men are simply psychological constructs representing people's desire to be free of the restraints of society. Another theory contends that the wild men were people suffering from hypertrichosis, a rare condition in which long hair grows all over the body. For their part, some cryptozoologists hypothesize that the Wudewása may have been neither mythical nor human, but a real animal—perhaps a member of an unknown species of hairy biped similar to the Florida Skunk Ape or the better-known Himalayan Yeti. Unlike those creatures, however, Europe's wild man has not been sighted since the Middle Ages.

For three years during the eighteenth century, an equally mysterious, but still more frightening, creature terrorized just one small section of the European continent: a remote mountainous region of south-central France known as Gévaudan. The horror began in July 1764, when a young girl keeping watch over her family's livestock was found dead in an isolated summer pasture, her heart ripped from her body. Within a few days, several more children met similar tragic fates. Horrified parents quickly brought their children down from the mountain pastures, and the killings stopped. After a few weeks, the parents sent the children back up into the mountains to tend the cattle and sheep. Seemingly, life returned to normal.

But only for a short time. In late August, a woman from the village of Langogne reported seeing a remarkable and truly frightening creature: a beast as big as a donkey

The short ears and large teeth in this 1765 depiction of the Beast of Gévaudan match some early descriptions of the savage creature—although its expression seems surprisingly pleasant. Other accounts gave hoofs and a snout to the animal that terrorized south-central France until 1767.

The supposed Owlman of Cornwall soars on vast, batlike wings in this 1976 sketch by alleged eyewitness June Melling. As if drawn to worship, the creature invariably was reported near the town church in Mawnan (right), usually flying dozens of feet off the ground.

with a piglike snout, short reddish hair, tiny ears, and a long tail, which walked on its two hind legs like a man. The creature had chased her dogs away, the woman said, but had been frightened off by her cattle, which had threatened the strange beast with their horns.

Few believed the fantastic story until it was corroborated a few days later by the testimony of another witness, this time a man, who said he had fired at the beast with his musket. Soon after this report, the murders of children began again. The horrified people of Gévaudan now believed that a fierce *loup-garou,* or werewolf, had come to dwell in their mountains.

By February, word of the werewolf had reached King Louis XV, who dispatched a company of soldiers to Gévaudan to hunt down and kill the dread beast. Upon their arrival, the soldiers came across the creature almost immediately and shot at it. Although the animal escaped into the forest, the soldiers believed that enough of their bullets had hit the creature to fatally wound it. They reported as much to the king, who proclaimed the beast dead.

Unfortunately, the announcement proved premature. The following summer, more murdered children were found in the mountains. No further aid came from the capital that year, but in 1766, the king's soldiers returned to the district. This time they tracked down and killed a huge wolf, which they promptly declared to be the Beast of Gévaudan. Again, the king announced the crisis was over.

Once more, however, the soldiers had proved too confident of their success. In the spring of 1767, the murders began anew. Terrified residents abandoned their homes and moved their families to other villages, far from the monster's stalking grounds. Finally, in early June, a local nobleman gathered together a huge group of hunters and set out after the creature, vowing to return only when the animal was truly dead. On June 19, in a small wooded area near Le Sogne d'Auvert, the hunters found and surrounded their prey. One of the men, Jean Chastel, fired two silver bullets at the animal; the second pierced the beast's heart and it fell dead.

To reassure everyone that the terrible monster had

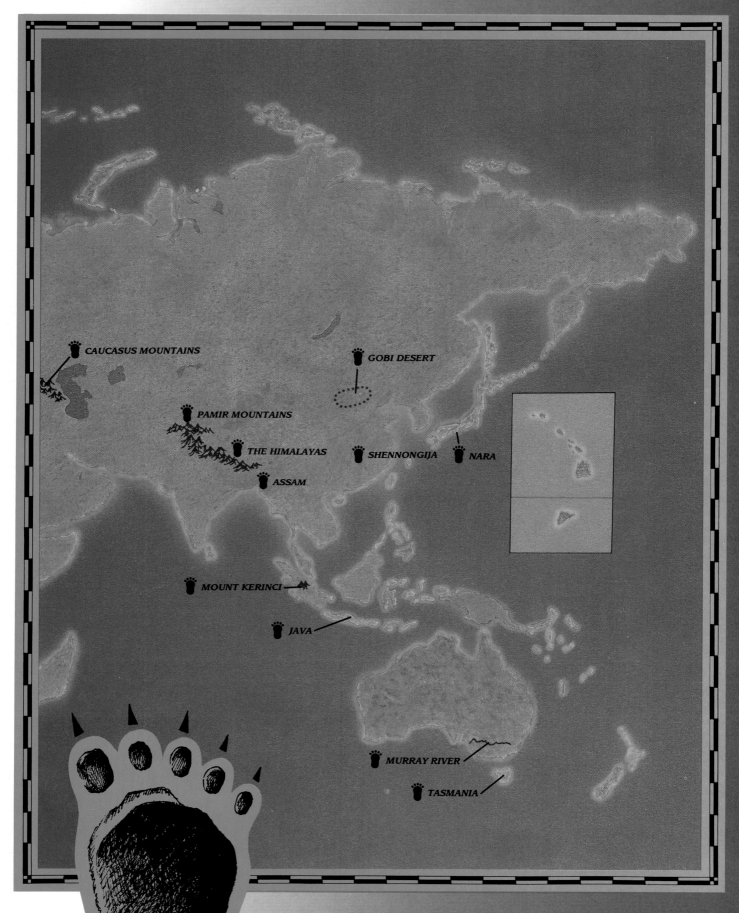

CAUCASUS MOUNTAINS

GOBI DESERT

PAMIR MOUNTAINS

THE HIMALAYAS

SHENNONGIJA

NARA

ASSAM

MOUNT KERINCI

JAVA

MURRAY RIVER

TASMANIA

really been killed, the triumphant hunters paraded the animal's carcass through the villages of Gévaudan. Unfortunately, only vague descriptions and widely varying sketches of the dead animal have survived. No further scientific study is possible, since there is no record of where the creature was buried. The people of Gévaudan, however, can still point to the spot where Jean Chastel is said to have killed the beast, and the valiant hunter's gun occupies a place of honor in the village church of Saint Martin-de-Bouchaux.

What kind of creature was the Beast of Gévaudan? Despite the extraordinary carnage it left behind, many believe the beast was simply a particularly large and ferocious wolf, or perhaps several wolves with rabies, a disease that could have caused the animals to attack humans. Others think the real murderer was not an animal at all, but a serial killer, who may have coincidentally died—or chosen to break off the killings—at about the time Chastel shot the wolf. Still others hold to the old peasant belief that the beast was both human and animal—a werewolf that could change from one form to the other at will.

If that beast is dead, however, other elusive creatures may still be flourishing in southern Europe—including, say some, that ancient legendary terror, the dragon. Linked to the nineteenth-century Swedish Lindorm and sighted not only in Britain but also in Bologna, Italy, in the 1600s, a dragon was supposedly seen as recently as 1970 in the woods near Forlì in central Italy. In

A flying elephant from a Ming dynasty cup

July of that year, forty-eight-year-old farm worker Antonio Samorani said he had been chased by "an enormous scaley thing at least four and a half meters long. It moved on large paws and its breath was fiery. I ran off at speed and it followed me for almost 200 meters." Police were at first skeptical but then reportedly found large footprints that seemed to bear out the story. There the tale ends, although the enigma continues. If not a dragon, what was it that pursued Samorani and left those footprints? And where did it go?

Although few if any dragon sightings have been reported in recent times in Asia and the neighboring Pacific, that vast part of the globe may be populated with any of a number of rumored, highly elusive creatures, including the Himalayan Yeti. Less publicized, but more wide-ranging, is a central Asian cousin of the Yeti that is commonly known by the Mongolian name Almas. The tall, hairy Almas has been reported in so many parts of Asia that there are more than forty different local names for the beast.

Some of the most persistent of these extraordinary reports have come from Tadzhikistan, a central Asian republic of the former Soviet Union, where remote, glacier-topped peaks of the Pamir Mountains reach heights of more than 20,000 feet.

Documented sightings of Almas date back to the early 1400s and continued into the twentieth century. In 1925, for instance, Major General Mikhail Topilsky and his Red Army troops reportedly killed an Almas accidentally while engaged in a gun battle with White Army forces in a part of the Pamir Mountains. "At first I

SECRET ANIMALS OF ASIA AND THE PACIFIC

ASSAM
Twelve feet long with rows of short spikes along its back, the elusive reptilian Buru is said to have inhabited swamps in this remote province of India. According to local tradition, it had blue and white skin.

THE HIMALAYAS
In these frozen Asian peaks allegedly dwells the humanoid Yeti, sometimes called the Abominable Snowman. Despite age-old stories and occasional modern sightings, the Yeti's existence has yet to be proved.

JAVA
Named for its reputed cry, a haunting howl, the giant, bat-like Athol supposedly ranges through the forested mountains of this Pacific island. Despite its size, the shy creature is said to avoid human beings.

MOUNT KERINCI
In 1989, tracks some identified as those of the Orang Pendek, a supposed humanoid, were found near this active Sumatran volcano. Sightings of the beast have been reported for centuries on Sumatra.

MURRAY RIVER
This Australian river is one of many rumored habitats of the carnivorous Bunyip, also reported on the neighboring island of TASMANIA. According to legend, the monster stalks people and other prey at night.

NARA
Long a part of Japanese folklore, the plump but speedy Tzuchinoko snake was reported near this city in 1987. Modern sightings are so numerous that some have called the beast the Loch Ness monster of Japan.

PAMIR MOUNTAINS
An Asian man-beast known as the Almas has often been reported sighted in this mountain range as well as in the CAUCASUS MOUNTAINS and in the GOBI DESERT.

SHENNONGIJA
Between 1976 and 1978, nearly a hundred Chinese scientists aided by army units searched mountains near this village for the Wildman, a hairy humanoid reported for centuries. The hunt proved unsuccessful.

Based on the alleged eyewitness account of a Kazakh herdsman, this drawing by Russian zoologist V. A. Khakhlov apparently depicts a tired Almas at rest in the fetal position.

thought it was the corpse of an ape," said General Topilsky of this odd casualty. "It was covered with fur. But I knew there were no apes in the Pamirs, and, moreover, the body looked far more human than ape-like, indeed, fully human." Although the dead creature was potentially a spectacular scientific find, the embattled troops could not take the body with them. They left it in the mountains, buried under a pile of stones.

In August 1957 Soviet hydrologist Alexander G. Pronin supposedly stumbled upon another Almas during a scientific expedition to study the water resources of the Pamir Mountains. As Pronin was following the course of the Balyandkiik River, he later said, he noticed a humanoid figure with a very hunched back standing between 500 and 600 yards away on the snow-covered southern slope of the valley. Pronin said that at first he took it to be a bear. "But then I saw it more clearly," he explained, "and realized that it was a manlike creature. It was walking on two feet, upright, but in a stooping fashion. It was quite naked, and its thickset body was covered with reddish hair."

Motivated by Pronin's tantalizing account, a group of prominent Soviet zoologists, archaeologists, botanists, and mountain climbers trekked into the Pamir Mountains two years later. After nine fruitless months of searching for the Almas, they gave up the quest and returned home.

In the years that followed, only a few Soviet scientists attempted to gather more evidence of these strange wild men of the mountains. In the 1950s and 1960s, a Russian historian and scientist named Boris Porshnev investigated hundreds of Almas stories, including that of a female Almas—named Zana by her human captors—who supposedly became a slave on a farm in the Caucasus. Porshnev concluded the Almas were modern relics of the original Neanderthals, the prehistoric humans who lived in what is now central Asia and Europe until about 40,000 years ago, when Cro-Magnon humans took their place.

In the 1980s, Russian anatomist and mountain climber Marie-Jeanne Koffmann added a sad postscript. Based on the dwindling number of sightings, she suggested the Almas may be on the verge of extinction, perhaps because of pressures put on its habitat by expanding human activity.

Just such a threatened man-beast may still wander the jungles of Sumatra, a Pacific island that straddles the equator thousands of miles to the south of the Pamir Mountains. For centuries, stories have been told on the island of small, shy creatures known as Orang Pendeks, or Little Men, who live deep in the island's tropical forests.

Sumatrans clearly distinguish between the orangutans of northeastern Sumatra and the Orang Pendeks, which are generally reported in the south. Orangutans (the name means "men of the woods") are ordinary reddish-brown apes, while Orang Pendeks are described as short, furry bipeds, about two to five feet in height, with striking manes of jet-black hair that run from their heads down to the middle of their backs. And unlike both apes and monkeys, which often move by swinging through the trees, Orang Pendeks are reported to travel by walking on the ground.

Fourteenth-century explorer Marco Polo was the first European to write about Sumatra's Orang Pendeks, who he asserted had tails "like those of the dog, but not covered with hair"—a detail not mentioned in modern accounts. Despite that early endorsement, however, Western naturalists tended to dismiss the Orang Pendek as a mythical beast until the early twentieth century, when several Dutch settlers reported close encounters with the creature that indigenous Sumatrans had been reporting for centuries.

In 1923, a settler named van Herwaarden said he saw an Orang Pendek while hunting wild pig on the island of Poeloe Rimau in the Banyuasin River of eastern Sumatra. Near dusk, he said, he spotted movement in a small tree. Van Herwaarden then crept toward the tree, where he discovered "a dark and hairy creature on a branch, the front of its body pressed tightly against the tree. It looked as if it were trying to make itself inconspicuous and felt that it was about to be discovered."

Van Herwaarden observed that the creature was five feet tall, apparently female, and had a brown, hairless face under a heap of shaggy, waist-length hair. Its eyes and ears seemed very human, he said, but not its teeth, which were large and well-developed. The animal was obviously terrified of being seen by a human—and with good reason, for when the beast finally dropped from the tree to flee, the Dutchman raised his gun to shoot it. Something kept him from firing the gun, however. "Many people may think me childish if I say that when I saw its flying hair in the sights I did not pull the trigger," he wrote. "I suddenly felt that I was going to commit murder."

In the years that followed, offers of large rewards encouraged others to bring dead Orang Pendeks out of the Sumatran jungle. Or so it was claimed; upon examination, the crop of specimens all proved to be hoaxes. In the last of these sorry episodes, in 1932, four Sumatrans handed scientists the body of what they said was a newborn Orang Pendek. It turned out to be a common Sumatran monkey known as a lotong. To make the monkey look like the

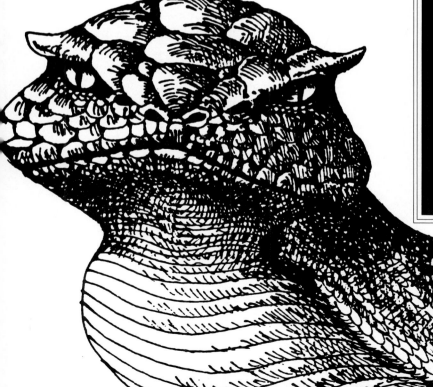

An Elusive Supersnake

Few natural environments have been as carefully studied as that of Japan, yet reports persist of at least one creature there that has so far eluded scientific scrutiny. As shown in the artist's conception at the bottom of this page and overleaf, the Tzuchinoko is said to be a pudgy snake with a hypnotic stare. When not occupied in glaring at passing humans, the beast reportedly travels in a characteristically odd way. Several observers have claimed to see it leap as far as six feet *(small diagram, below);* others say the Tzuchinoko can curl into a hoop to roll down hills.

Mentioned in Japanese folk tales for centuries, the Tzuchinoko has often been reported in modern times. When alleged sightings occur, local politicians frequently respond by forming "animal research associations" to search for the Tzuchinoko—and to attract visitors to their towns. One such hunt in April 1988 was triggered by two claimed Tzuchinoko sightings in the vicinity of Nara, Japan. Accompanied by more than eighty reporters and photographers, the eager monster hunters pounded sticks under tea plants, raked leaves in forests, and beat on wooden structures to scare out Tzuchinokos—all to no avail.

Since similar searches take place year after year somewhere in Japan with no success, skeptics have cause to doubt that the Tzuchinoko exists. Most zoologists dismiss the creature as a myth, on grounds that inexperienced observers have probably seen a common viper engaged in uncommon behavior. But other researchers—and many alleged witnesses—vehemently disagree, and the periodic Tzuchinoko hunts testify to their enduring faith in the leaping snake.

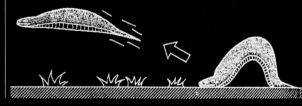

legendary Orang Pendek, its captors had shaved all the hair off the animal's body except on its head and had crushed its cheekbones and reshaped its nose.

Put off by such incidents, most zoologists now believe the Orang Pendek is simply a myth inspired by encounters with other animals on the island, such as the *bruan,* a small black bear that stands about five feet tall on its hind legs, or the gibbon, a small ape. Some cryptozoologists, however, question whether the people of Sumatra would so consistently misidentify animals as well known to them as the bruan or gibbon; these researchers suggest that instead the Orang Pendek may be an as-yet-unknown species of ape.

In 1990, more evidence to support that view, and perhaps confound the skeptics, was brought forward by Deborah Martyr, a British writer who first heard of the beast while traveling on the island in the summer of 1989. Martyr was not lucky enough to see an Orang Pendek herself, she reported, but she did find a series of footprints, small and human-shaped but much wider than a normal human foot. Martyr also commented that local reports of the Orang Pendek differed from tradition in that the beast was said to be pudgy rather than slender. A possible explanation of the latter change lay in the fact that all but one of the sightings Martyr was told about involved an Orang Pendek eating sugarcane in the local fields.

Remote Pacific islands apparently furnish good home grounds for mysterious creatures of many types, perhaps because so much of their forests remains unsettled and essentially untouched. Less than two miles to the east of Sumatra, the lush volcanic island of Java is said to be inhabited by another animal enigma, in this case a peculiar flying creature known as the Athol. A shy beast that reportedly lives in the caves along Java's riverbanks, the Athol received its name from the haunting sound it makes: ah-OOooool. The Athol is said to have a flat, monkeylike face and a small furry body, no bigger than that of a year-old baby, which is dwarfed by a wingspan of at least twelve feet. The Athol reportedly sometimes turns its feet backward, a trait that is said for unknown reasons to aid it in scooping fish from local rivers.

Putting the Athol's many characteristics together, cryptozoologists have concluded the Athol may be an unknown giant bat. Bats are the only recognized fur-covered flying animals, and their feet point backward to enable them to hang upside down. But only small, insect-eating bats are known to have flat faces, leaving the fish-eating Athol a perplexing zoological mystery for the time being.

Southeast of Java, across the Timor Sea, a veritable zoo of mysterious creatures has been linked to the massive island continent of Australia, which is also home to a number of scientifically recognized but anomalous creatures ranging from the duckbill and the echidna to a whole series of pouch-bearing marsupials.

Among the creatures not so well accepted is a monstrous rainbow-colored snake known as the Mindi, which is said to inhabit the lower Murray River in southeastern Australia, killing anyone who so much as glances at it. From farther in Australia's interior come stories of a horrifying creature called the Yara-ma-yha-who, a toothless froglike man whose fingers end in large suckers and who feeds on human blood. Other Australian stories tell of the Yahoo, or Yowie, a man-beast that is the Outback equivalent of the Almas.

None of Australia's elusive creatures is better known, however, than the Bunyip, whose name, derived from the aboriginal word for "devil" or "spirit," has become synonymous in Australia with any kind of mysterious beast. By most accounts, the creature is a large furry animal, about the size of a dog, with a head similar to that of a dog or kangaroo and very small ears. Like the Argentine Water-tiger, the Bunyip is said to be a mammal that likes water. According to Australian tradition, it swims with fins, lives in rivers, marshes, and lakes, and emits a loud, hideous cry.

That piercing sound looms large in the first documented report of a Bunyip, made in June 1801 by French explorer Charles Bailly. As he and his crew sailed inland from Australia's western coast on what is now called the Swan River, Bailly reported, they suddenly heard a terrible roar, louder than a bull's, rise up from the river's reedy depths. Terrified, the sailors fled to the open sea, bringing the first European-Bunyip encounter to an abrupt close.

Two decades later, in 1821, the Australian explorer Hamilton Hume told the members of a philosophical society at a meeting in Sydney that he had seen the water monster in Lake Bathurst in what is now the state of New South Wales. Hume never earned the reward that the society then offered for a skull or other evidence of the unknown animal.

But in 1846, an Australian naturalist was loaned a strange piece of a skull that had been discovered on the banks of the Murrumbidgee River, a tributary of the Murray. Local Aborigines said that it came from the skeleton of a Bunyip. An expert who examined the skull fragment, however, thought it more likely to be from the deformed skull of a young horse. A drawing of the bone was later sent to the British anatomist Sir Richard Owen, who pronounced it to be that of a calf. Unfortunately, the specimen later disappeared from the Australian Museum, so the question

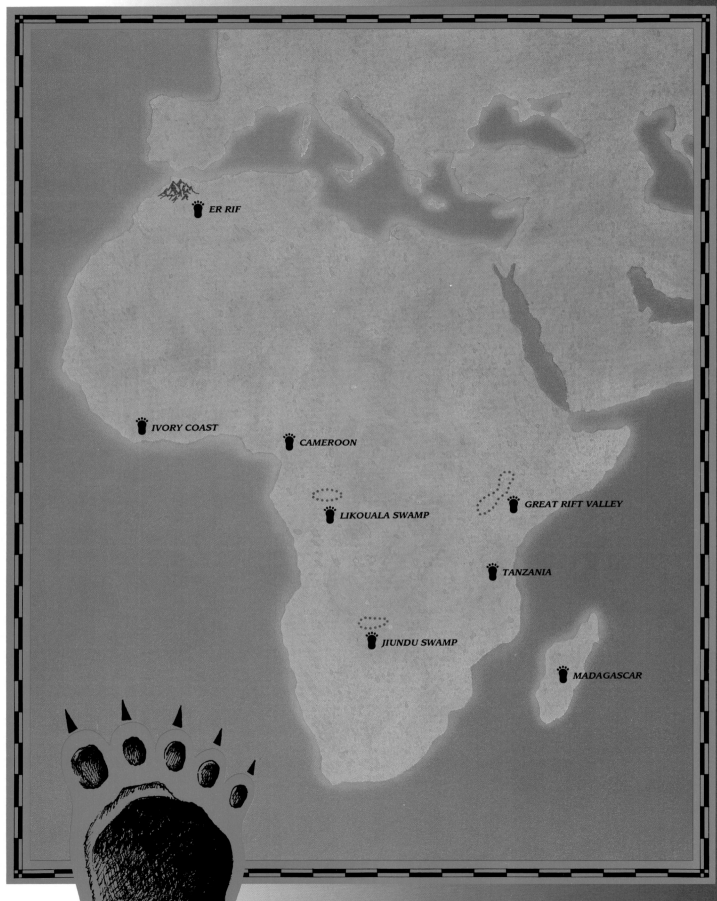

ER RIF

IVORY COAST

CAMEROON

LIKOUALA SWAMP

GREAT RIFT VALLEY

TANZANIA

JIUNDU SWAMP

MADAGASCAR

of the skull's precise identity may never be resolved.

Reports of the Bunyip continued, however, particularly in southeastern Australia. In 1848, a Bunyip was allegedly seen swimming in the Eumerall River in Victoria. Witnesses described the creature as a large brown animal with a hairy mane, an enormous mouth, and a head like a kangaroo. In 1872, a boatman on Lake Corangamite in Victoria similarly reported seeing an "animal like a big retriever dog, with a round head and hardly any ears." The man was so terrified by the creature that he overturned his punt.

By 1890, Bunyip sightings had become so numerous that the Melbourne Zoo sent a team of hunters into the Eurora district of Victoria to try to capture a specimen for their collection. The group returned empty-handed. Yet half a century later reports of the elusive creature kept rolling in, with a sighting by several people in 1943 in the Great Lake of Tasmania. In May 1965 a group of hunters went looking for Bunyips in the Nerang River in southeast Queensland after local farmers told of hearing unearthly roars and seeing strange movements in the water.

Not all observers believe in the Bunyip; indeed, the term "Bunyip aristocracy" was coined in the late nineteenth century to ridicule attempts to create an Australian order of nobility—

Many-headed beast, Middle East

no more genuine, it was implied, than the mythical Bunyip. Many skeptics believe that Bunyips are simply marine mammals that have strayed too far inland along Australia's rivers. In fact, seals and sea lions have been spotted in Australia's rivers as far as 900 miles from the sea. But other Bunyip reports come from places that even the most adventurous seal or sea lion could not reach. Some suggest those accounts might be inspired by aboriginal memories of an unknown marsupial otterlike animal, now apparently extinct. Although that explanation fails to account for modern sightings, it remains a possibility, since no direct evidence of a Bunyip has ever been produced.

For all the interest cryptozoologists take in the Australian Bunyip or the central Asian Almas, Asia and the Pacific are not the core hunting grounds of their discipline. That distinction must be left to Africa, and especially to its vast central rain forest, one of the most fecund wilderness areas left on earth. Africa is close to ideal for eager cryptozoologists. "As it is almost impossible to penetrate this dense, dark and unhealthy jungle without disturbing the shy creatures that inhabit it," wrote Bernard Heuvelmans in his 1955 book *On the Track of Unknown Animals,* "many of them may live there without our having the least chance

AFRICA'S UNKNOWN CREATURES

CAMEROON
A large, black bat known locally as the Olitiau is believed to inhabit the mountains of this nation. The Olitiau may be the same as the Kongamato (see JIUNDU SWAMP); both have been reported by hunters but have never been captured.

ER RIF
Bordering the Mediterranean, this hilly region of Morocco is rumored to shelter a species of dwarfish bears—despite zoologists' accepted view that there are no wild bears in Africa.

GREAT RIFT VALLEY
The Kenyan portion of this vast, continent-spanning chasm is one reputed refuge of the Nandi Bear. Unrecognized by science, the supposed predator is said to eat the brains of its prey.

IVORY COAST
In the forests of this country reputedly live small, red-haired humanoids called Séhités, equivalent to the Agogwe of Tanzania. Supposedly, the Séhités bring bad luck to those who see them.

JIUNDU SWAMP
Situated in northwestern Zambia, these wetlands are allegedly home to the Kongamato, an elusive but ferocious giant bat. In the past, local residents carried a charmed bundle of bark to ward off the beast's attacks.

LIKOUALA SWAMP
A large, claw-footed reptile known as Mokele-mbembe supposedly roams this area of the Congo. Some researchers propose the creature may be a small sauropod dinosaur that somehow escaped extinction.

MADAGASCAR
This vast island was once home to a huge, flightless fowl known as the elephant bird. Standing ten feet tall and weighing half a ton, the creature may have inspired tales of the fabulously big Roc.

TANZANIA
Petite, red-haired hominids known as Agogwe purportedly live in this country and in its southern neighbor Mozambique. The beings allegedly resemble the australopithecines, a prehuman genus thought to be long extinct.

Cloaked in low-lying clouds, Kenya's Great Rift Valley is a frequent setting for reports of the predatory Nandi Bear. According to British big-game hunter Charles T. Stoneham (left), who searched fruitlessly for the beast in the 1920s, the Nandi Bear often attacked its human victims by breaking through the roofs of their huts.

of meeting them except in exceptional circumstances."

Not all of these unknown animals are said to be shy, however. The east African nation of Kenya has long been the rumored home of a bearlike beast so savage and fearless that it supposedly visits villages at night, carrying off sheep and sometimes people. European settlers named the creature the Nandi Bear, after the people in whose territory, located in the far west of Kenya, it has been most often seen. But the native peoples of Kenya have other, more ominous names for the beast, including Chemosit, or devil, and Geteit, which means brain eater—a reference to the beast's alleged habit of eating only the brain of its prey.

"Men told me it came down to the villages at night and murdered the inhabitants in their huts," wrote well-known big-game hunter Charles T. Stoneham, who described his own turn-of-the-century search for the Nandi Bear in his 1933 book *Hunting Wild Beasts with Rifle and Camera*. "It made its entrance through the roof, killed the occupants, and ate their brains." Women who were out in the forest collecting wood "would be missed," Stoneham went on, "and later their bodies would be discovered, always minus the tops of their skulls."

Because no species of bear is known to exist in Africa—although there are persistent rumors, dismissed by most scientists, of small bears in Morocco—the reports of the Nandi Bear have puzzled zoologists. Yet the term "bear" seems fitting, judging by many reports. Geoffrey Williams, an adventurer who explored Nandi territory at the beginning of the century, definitely thought the beast looked bearlike when he encountered it while hiking on the grassy Uasin-Gishu plateau. "There was a thick mist," he wrote, "and my cousin and I were walking on ahead of the safari." Suddenly the mist cleared. "My cousin called out 'What is that?' Looking in the direction to which he pointed I saw a large animal sitting up on its haunches not more than 30 yards away. Its attitude was just that of a bear at the

'Zoo' asking for buns, and I should say it must have been nearly 5 feet high,'' Williams recalled. "Before we had time to do anything it dropped forward and shambled away.''

In 1925, in an incident reminiscent of the eighteenth-century French terror of the Beast of Gévaudan, the inhabitants of one village asked the Kenyan government for help after a six-year-old girl was reportedly carried off in the night by a Nandi Bear that had torn a hole through the mud wall of her family's hut. On earlier nights, the creature had also dragged away several of the villagers' cattle. Captain William Hichens, a British colonial official, traveled to the town to investigate.

After listening to the terrified residents' accounts of the raids, Hichens decided to trap the beast by encircling its suspected location on a small, forested hill. The plan failed, but Hichens did have a frightening encounter with what he thought was the same creature one night after he had gone to bed in a tent he had set up near the village. "I had a small khaki-coloured pi-dog named Mbwambi with me, a mongrel, but a ferocious, plucky, little beast, and I tied him up to the door of my tent,'' Hichens wrote two years after the incident. "It was well after midnight when he gave a sharp, alarmed, whiny growl and woke me. But before I could get out of bed the whole tent rocked; the pole to which Mbwambi was tied flew out and let down the ridge-pole, enveloping me in a flapping canvas. At the same moment the most awful howl I have ever heard split the night. The sheer demoniac horror of it froze me still.

I heard my pi-dog yelp just once,'' Hichens chillingly continued. "There was a crashing of branches in the bush, and then thud, thud, thud of some huge beast making off. But that howl! I have heard half a dozen lions roaring in a stampede chorus not twenty yards away; I have heard a maddened cow-elephant trumpeting; I have heard a trapped leopard make the silent night a rocking agony with screaming, snarling roars. But never have I heard, nor do I wish to hear again, such a howl as that of the chimiset.''

Hichens raced outside, where he found his dog gone and a trail of blood leading into the jungle. Next to the trail were huge footprints, "four times as big as a man's,'' Hichens noted. At daybreak, he and a hunting party from the village tracked the footprints into the forest, but after a week, the trail grew cold. Hichens never found the animal whose howl had caused his very soul to shudder.

Many scientists believe that those who say they have sighted the Nandi Bear have simply misidentified a known animal, such as a hyena, a baboon, or a ratel (a nocturnal carnivorous mammal that resembles a badger and is found in Africa, Arabia, and India). But at least one expert, Charles Williams, formerly of the British Museum of Natural History, has proposed a more startling theory. He suggests that the Nandi Bear might be a living descendant of a peculiar prehistoric group of mammals known as the Chalicotheria. These odd-looking creatures, distantly related to modern horses, had short hind legs, sloping backs, heavy square-snouted heads, short tails, and formidable claws. Just when they became extinct is not known, although paleontologists believe it was at least 10,000 years ago.

Unexpected survival from the past may also explain

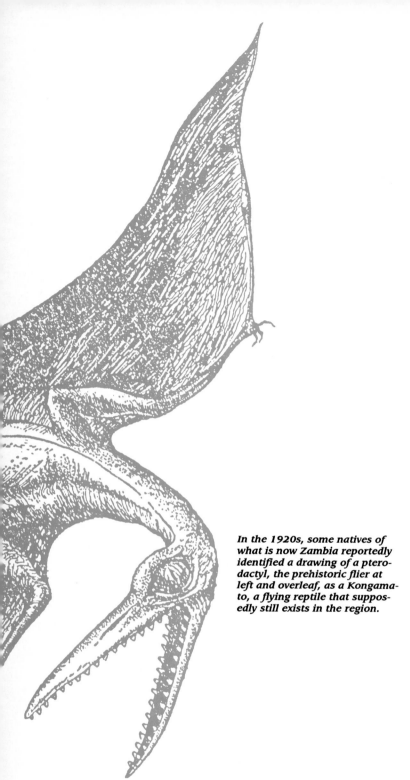

In the 1920s, some natives of what is now Zambia reportedly identified a drawing of a pterodactyl, the prehistoric flier at left and overleaf, as a Kongamato, a flying reptile that supposedly still exists in the region.

the Agogwe, a short, human-faced creature covered in red hair that has been reported in remote sections of Mozambique and Tanzania. Captain Hichens, the man who attempted to catch a Nandi Bear, reported that he once came across two Agogwe while tracking down a man-killing lion in the dense jungle forests of Tanzania's Wembere plains.

"While waiting in a forest glade," Hichens recalled, "I saw two small, brown, furry creatures come from the dense forest on one side of the glade and disappear into the thickets on the other. They were like little men, about four feet high, walking upright, but clad in russet hair. The native hunter with me gazed in mingled fear and amazement. They were, he said, *agogwe,* the little furry men whom one does not see once in a lifetime."

In 1938, the British journal *Discovery* published a letter from a man named Cuthbert Burgoyne that described a similar sighting of two Agogwe. The incident took place in 1927, Burgoyne wrote, while he and his wife were traveling in a Japanese cargo boat along the coast of what is now Mozambique. They had taken out their binoculars one afternoon to watch a group of baboons hunting shellfish and crabs on a beach, when two apparent Agogwe "walked together out of the bush and down amongst the baboons," Burgoyne recalled. "They were too far away to see in detail, but these small human-like animals were probably between four and five feet tall, quite upright and graceful in figure. At the time I was thrilled as they were quite evidently no beast of which I had heard or read."

Although most reports of the Agogwe have come from Africa's eastern coast, small red-haired, humanlike creatures have also been seen across the continent, in the tropical forests of the Ivory Coast. During the late 1940s, Professor A. Ledoux, then head of the Institute of Education and Research at Adiopodoumé near Abidjan, collected many stories from Africans and from European travelers of "little men" with long reddish fur who were believed to live in the jungles of the interior. One European hunter said he had killed such a creature in the dense forested area between the Sassandra and Cavally rivers in 1947. Unfortunately, while the hunter was bringing the strange animal out of the jungle, his African porters disposed of it, perhaps because of a local belief that the Agogwe brings horrible luck.

Just who are these reclusive furry creatures—if they exist at all? Apes and monkeys have been ruled out, for they do not usually walk upright on their hind legs. Nor do the Agogwe match any known human type. Because of their stature, they have been compared to Pygmies or San people, but both groups of small humans live far from the Agogwe's alleged haunts and do not have red hair, among other physical dissimilarities.

Instead, some cryptozoologists propose, the "little hairy men" of Africa may be surviving representatives of a gnomish race known to paleontologists as *Australopithecus.* About five feet tall, with a brain intermediate in size between those of modern apes and those of human beings, the australopithecines inhabited southern and eastern Africa beginning about 8 million years ago. They are believed to have walked erect and to have used simple stone tools. Scientists are not sure when the australopithecines became extinct, although some believe it may have been as recently as 1.5 million years ago—possibly at the hands of more aggressive hominids. Perhaps, some cryptozoologists speculate, a few australopithecines retreated to the secluded safety of Africa's densely forested interior.

Not all the mysterious creatures supposedly hidden in the thick African forests are mammals, of course. There are reports of strange birds as well. Perhaps the best known of these is the Roc, a seemingly fantastical bird first described in Middle Eastern tales dating back to at least the ninth century AD. A monstrous bird that reportedly fed elephants to its young, the Roc—or Rukh, as it is sometimes called—was said to inhabit the African island of Madagascar. According to some ancient stories, the creature was so strong that it once sank a ship by dropping huge boulders on it.

Although most of what has been written about the Roc is obviously mythological or fanciful, the creature was probably inspired by a gigantic bird that really did exist in Madagascar—*Aepyornis maximus,* the elephant bird. One of the largest birds that ever lived, it looked like a huge ostrich and laid eggs equal in size to about 150 chicken eggs. Almost certainly extinct now, the elephant bird may have survived into the sixteenth century, according to some cryptozoologists. If so, hunters probably brought about its demise. The creature's huge feathers and eggs would have brought good money for traders in far-off lands.

Tales of huge flying creatures, from the African Roc to the British Owlman and the American Thunderbird, seem to come naturally to humankind, perhaps because such mysterious creatures range so widely they are more likely to be seen—or perhaps because of instinctive human fears of airborne predators that date to our most distant past. Almost invariably, the flying menace is associated with thick wood-

Carrying off an elephant in the woodcut at left, the enormous Roc featured in Middle Eastern legends may have been based on a real animal: the huge, flightless elephant bird, which once inhabited Madagascar.

lands, in which it can perch concealed until its next attack.

Just such a creature has been reported in several regions of Africa, including the Jiundu swamp of northwestern Zambia. The Kongamato, as it is known, is usually described as a lizard-bird with a four- to seven-foot wingspan and a huge beak full of teeth. The Kongamato has a murderous reputation among Zambians, who say the creature can make a canoe capsize.

Colonel C. R. S. Pitman, a longtime game warden in Uganda, wrote about the legendary Kongamato in 1942, twelve years after he learned of it as a captain stationed in what is now Zambia. "I heard of a mythical beast which intrigued me considerably," he recalled. "To look upon it is death. But the most amazing feature of this mystery beast is its suggested identity with a creature bat-bird-like in form on a gigantic scale strangely reminiscent of the prehistoric pterodactyl."

The Kongamato's resemblance to a pterodactyl, one of the pterosaurs, or winged lizards, that existed during the Mesozoic era about 160 million years ago, has intrigued cryptozoologists. Could the Kongamato be one of these ancient flying reptiles? Reports of the Kongamato diving at boats has lent credence to this belief, for many paleontologists believe some pterodactyls had such abilities.

The most dramatic account of a Kongamato came not from Zambia, however, but from Cameroon, some 1,100 miles to the northwest, where the creature is known as an Olitiau. The incident was reported by a British naturalist and zoologist named Ivan Sanderson, who led an expedition into the Assumbo mountains of Cameroon in 1932. While wading among the rocks of a steep-banked river one afternoon, Sanderson shot and killed what he thought was a large fruit-eating bat, which dropped into the water. As he tried to retrieve the bat's carcass, Sanderson slipped and fell into the river. He was struggling to get back to shore, when another member of the expedition named George Russell suddenly shouted, "Look out!"

"I looked," Sanderson later wrote. "Then I let out a shout also and instantly bobbed down under the water, because, coming straight at me only a few feet above the water was a black thing the size of an eagle. I had only a glimpse of its face, yet that was quite sufficient, for its lower jaw hung open and bore a semicircle of pointed white teeth set about their own width apart from each other."

Russell shot at the beast, Sanderson said, which then flew off across the sky and disappeared. Sanderson pulled himself out of the water, his body shaking from the incident, wondering if the creature would return. It did, just before nightfall. "It came again, hurtling back down the river, its teeth chattering, the air 'shss-shssing' as it was cleft by the great, black, dracula-like wings," Sanderson recalled. "We were both off our guard, my gun was unloaded, and the brute made straight for George. He ducked. The animal soared over him and was at once swallowed up in the night." When the two men returned to their camp that night, they asked several local African hunters about the flying beast. The men told them it was an Olitiau.

Although Sanderson did not attempt to identify the creature that attacked him and his companion, he described it as looking like a gigantic bat. As a result, some observers have suggested that the Kongamato or Olitiau may be a large unidentified type of hammerhead bat, a creature that has wide-spaced teeth and sometimes flies low over water. Hammerhead bats are usually docile creatures, not known to attack humans. The animal that attacked Sanderson, however, did so right after he had shot a large bat. Perhaps the creature was acting in an unusual manner in an attempt to protect its injured mate.

Like many another account in the frustrating field of cryptozoology, Sanderson's story, in the end, yields more questions than answers. As long as earth retains unexplored nooks and crannies, the possibility of unacknowledged inhabitants in mountains, lakes, and jungle lands will remain. Whether it is a pterodactyl, a new form of hammerhead bat, or a creature yet unknown to science, the puzzle of the Kongamato is still to be solved, as are the mysteries surrounding a number of remote regions of the planet and the enigmatic creatures rumored to live there.

Tales from the Deep

The crew of U.S. Navy vessel AFB-14 had never seen anything like it. Finishing up a stint of oceanographic research near Hawaii on a November afternoon in 1976, they hauled in their sea anchors to find a monstrous and unidentifiable shark mortally entangled in one of them. The mysterious fish was 14.5 feet long and weighed some 1,650 pounds. Even more distinctive than its enormity was its mouth—the size of a small bathtub and lined with 484 needlelike teeth. The beast quickly earned the nickname Megamouth. Scientists classified it as the only known member of an entirely new family of sharks.

The discovery of the Megamouth underscored the fact that there still lurk in the depths of the sea creatures totally unknown to humankind. Indeed, modern science is comparatively ignorant of marine life because earth's vast oceans remain largely unexplored. Thus the reports of people who say they have seen strange denizens of the deep cannot be dismissed out of hand. In a few cases, sightings by nonexperts have even helped scientists to identify new kinds of marine life. Scandinavian sailors, for instance, had long reported a large tentacled sea monster they called the kraken. Scientists dismissed the claims as imaginary—until the second half of the nineteenth century, when repeated sightings and beached specimens finally convinced them to recognize the creature as real and classify it as *Architeuthis dux,* the giant squid.

In hopes that other sea monster allegations might also be validated, French cryptozoologist Bernard Heuvelmans has investigated all such reports documented between 1639 and 1965. After rejecting clear cases of mistaken identity and obvious hoaxes—such as a creature spotted at a latitude and longitude that placed it in the deserts of Libya—Heuvelmans was left with 358 apparently credible claims. These he grouped by their descriptions into the following categories: the merhorse (a maned, equinelike creature); the marine saurian (a crocodile-like beast); the father-of-all-the-turtles (a huge tortoise); the superotter; the yellow-belly; and sea serpents classified variously as long-necked, many-humped, many-finned, and the supereel. Some of the reports that Heuvelmans investigated are described on these pages, with the locations of the sightings shown on a world map. The old illustrations depict creatures of the deep—some real, some imaginary, and some whose existence or lack of it has yet to be determined.

Churning the sea, a gigantic, ferociously coiling sea serpent challenges two whaleboats and a sailing ship in this 1862 drawing by French illustrator Gustave Doré. For centuries, Scandinavian sailors reported encounters with beasts like this one. Calling them sea worms, the men told fantastic tales of such serpents several hundred yards long, terrorizing seagoers with thunderous roars and "eyes that flashed lightning."

The mermaid and manatee above bear little resemblance to each other, but scientists have long suggested that reports of mermaids were actually sightings of these marine mammals, noted for their amiable faces.

French sailors attempt to capture a giant squid in this historical engraving. All they managed to catch was a chunk of the beast's tail, but it led to science's eventual recognition of the tentacled monster.

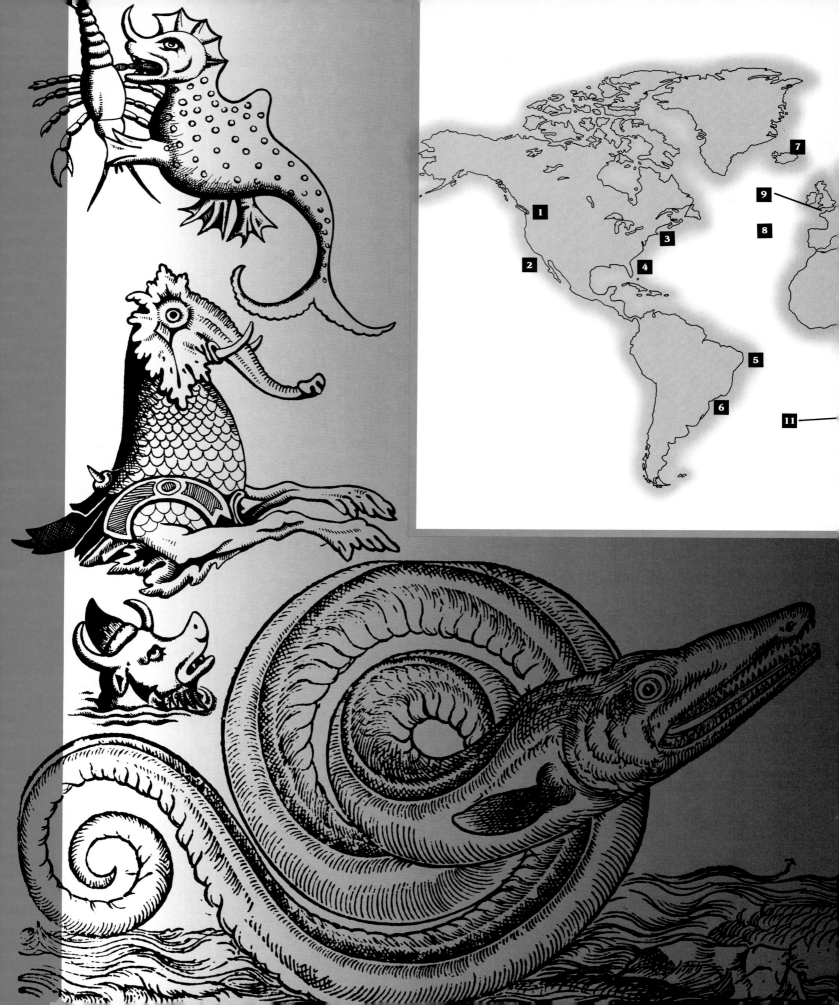

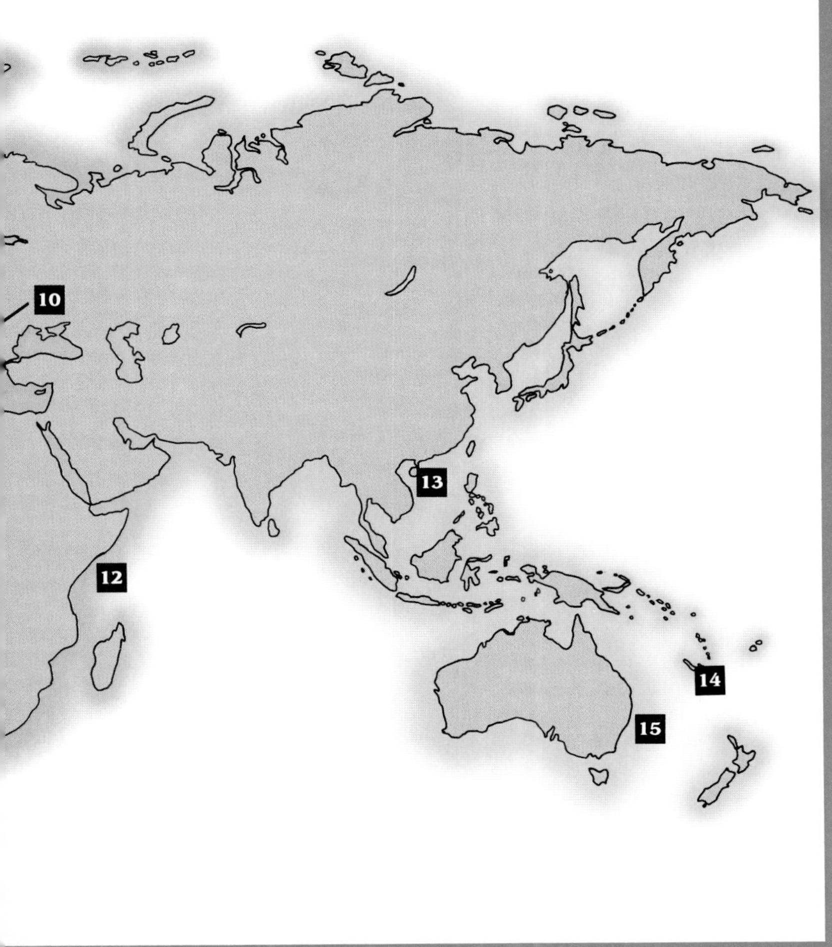

1

In Puget Sound and the neighboring Strait of Georgia, sea serpents have been reported since 1812. In 1984, a fisherman said he saw a twenty-foot creature with stubby, giraffelike horns and large floppy ears.

2

Numerous sea serpents have supposedly been seen in the Outer Santa Barbara Channel off southern California, including, in 1920, a monster with "a great columnar neck and head," a "mane of coarse hair like a fine seaweed," and eyes "a foot in diameter!"

3

In 1817, there were multiple sightings of a fifty-foot-long sea serpent with a large canine head in Gloucester Harbor, Massachusetts.

4

In 1896, a huge, octopus-like creature washed ashore at Anastasia Beach, Florida. And off Bermuda in 1984, commercial fishing traps were damaged by what cryptozoologists say may have been a giant octopus.

5

Cruising off the coast of Brazil in 1905, two British naturalists claimed to have spotted a long-necked serpent with a large dorsal fin and a turtlelike face.

6

In 1958, dozens of bathers and fishermen said they saw a humpbacked sea creature with a giraffelike neck and a green, barrel-size head in Guanabara Bay near Rio de Janeiro, Brazil.

7

Two men reported seeing a shiny black sea creature with two crests off the coast of Iceland in 1963. Another witness said he spotted the beast an hour later.

8

One of a two-man team rowing across the Atlantic in 1966 reported seeing "the writhing, twisting shape of a creature thirty-five or more feet long."

9

Morgawr—"sea giant" in Cornish—allegedly inhabits Falmouth Bay in Cornwall, England. People have reported seeing a many-humped, dark-skinned beast there since 1876, and a flurry of sightings occurred in the 1970s.

10

Tourists spearfishing off the coast of Grillone, Italy, in 1958 said they saw a gigantic eel-like creature. Other giant eel sightings were reported in the Mediterranean in 1912 and 1953.

11

Crew members of a ship rounding the Cape of Good Hope in 1948 claimed they saw a sixty-foot-long serpent. Dark brown with a yellowish throat and a seaweedlike mane, the creature moved fifteen miles per hour with no apparent means of propulsion.

12

A horned, broad-backed beast known to locals as the Kilindini sea monster supposedly frequents the strait between the island of Mombasa and the Kenyan mainland. Two Britons said they saw the creature in 1948.

13

In 1883 on Along Beach in Vietnam, a man claimed he found the decaying carcass of a huge millipede-like beast, with a segmented body and dozens of feet.

14

In 1923, two different sea serpents were reported in the South Pacific. The first was supposedly cork brown with a huge, thick body and a conical head; the second beast was a mahogany-colored merhorse with a crested head.

15

Crew members of a steamer passing through the coastal waters of eastern Australia in 1925 are said to have seen a yellowish, many-humped serpent with one large black fin and a swan neck.

CHAPTER 3

Where Energies Focus

F or the uninitiated, the boulder standing eleven feet high at one edge of a muddy field in Mission, British Columbia, was nothing more than a rock. A big rock, to be sure, but a rock nonetheless. Moreover, for the builder bent on converting the seventeen-acre field into a housing development, it was a rock in the wrong place—right in the path of progress.

Yet for the Indians of the local Sto:lo (pronounced "Stah-lo") tribe, who were calling this area home for thousands of years before anyone ever knew it as either Mission or British Columbia, the boulder is more than just a rock. It is Sma:alt Xath'aq (pronounced, approximately, "Smalt K'hat-sic," and commonly anglicized to Hatzic Rock), one of nearly 200 "ancestor stones" that dot Canada's Pacific coast. Trapped inside the rock, the Sto:lo believe, are the spirits of four chiefs, turned to stone by the god Xa:ls (pronounced "K'hals") for daring to ask for a written language.

Sma:alt Xath'aq became part of the tribe's sacred landscape and was subsequently revered by generations of Sto:lo. But sacred rocks and the spirits of long-dead Indians had little place in the new order imposed on the Sto:lo by Christian missionaries who arrived in the 1860s, and over the ensuing decades the rock and what it represented sank into obscurity.

That obscurity threatened to become oblivion late in 1990, as work on the new development began and Hatzic Rock was slated for demolition. Only the intervention of a local archaeologist named Gordon Mohs saved the day. Mohs alerted the owner of the land, Harry Utzig, to the rock's ancient significance and begged for time to further investigate the site. Utzig, whose interest in local history made him receptive to the appeal, temporarily halted the project and gave Mohs the time he had asked for.

Mohs and a team of volunteers went to work the following spring and soon unearthed the remains of two cedar-planked houses. Carbon-dated, the structures proved to be of astonishing antiquity, about 5,000 years old. Nearby were traces of other ancient buildings, ashes from a campfire that warmed its makers no less than 9,000 years ago, and thousands of artifacts older than Egypt's pyramids—the remains of an entire Indian village.

The finds spurred the community, much of it non-Indian, to redouble its efforts to save Hatzic Rock and its surroundings. At the same time, the rock's ancient power as a special place began to reemerge, as some 14,000 people came to pay their respects during the first year after its brush with imminent destruction. One was a music teacher convinced that this rock of ages had a story to tell—literally. Inspired by an Indian belief that a song was "trapped in the stone," he clambered up the rock at three o'clock one morning and there, all ears in the chill predawn stillness, he listened.

"I didn't hear a thing," the teacher later admitted. But the experience did move him to write his own song, one that soon became a fight song for Hatzic Rock's growing band of activists. Late in 1991 the government of British Columbia awarded the site a temporary "heritage" designation, further delaying the proposed housing development. Ironically, the government's action had the added effect of fueling the development plans of the Sto:lo tribal council itself, which hoped to make Hatzic Rock the centerpiece of a heritage park that would incorporate a museum and a reconstruction of one of the ancient houses.

As spiritual signpost and a repository of mystical power, Hatzic Rock has regained an honored place in a long roll of charmed spots around the world. Virtually every human culture has venerated its own Hatzic Rocks, sites that were—and are—recognized as sacred to the gods or revered as the abode of mysterious spirits, exalted for what the exalters see as inherent powers or treasured as memorials to some momentous events in the life of the culture.

And Hatzic Rock is now showing another trait common to places of power: the ability to work their apparently unquenchable magic on people who encounter them long after their special qualities were first recognized, often by cultures now gone and forgotten. Beginning far back in prehistoric times, such seemingly inanimate sites as springs and mountains—places where the energies

of the netherworld are believed to bubble to the surface or where the realms of earth and sky meet and mingle—have been viewed as conduits for those unexplained spiritual forces that seem to enliven all of nature.

With the emergence of religious ideas and the growing belief that life on earth may exist at the pleasure of unseen deities, mountains became the obvious setting for the dwelling places of those deities, springs and rivers the abodes of powerful spirits, and caves the places from which humans first emerged. Many of these same places also came to be seen as the points of intersection between the human world and the godly, as gateways to heaven, or even as rents in the veil that separates the living from the dead. As such, they often became places of pilgrimage, meccas toward which the faithful flocked in the hope of conversing with the gods or of communing with the departed.

Moreover, as the ruins of such hallowed places as Egypt's Karnak and the megalithic monuments of Europe so hauntingly show, places of power that nature failed to provide in the form of mountains and caves could be created. But they had to be located on sites whose power was inherent—human action alone could not make a place potent.

Although it was once believed that the entire earth was the domain of the gods, the boundaries of divine territory eventually began to shrink as people assumed greater control of the world around them, until at last the gods were corralled into temples, shrines, and tabernacles.

Invariably, as old religions gave way to new ones, the latter adopted the sacred places of the former. This was done

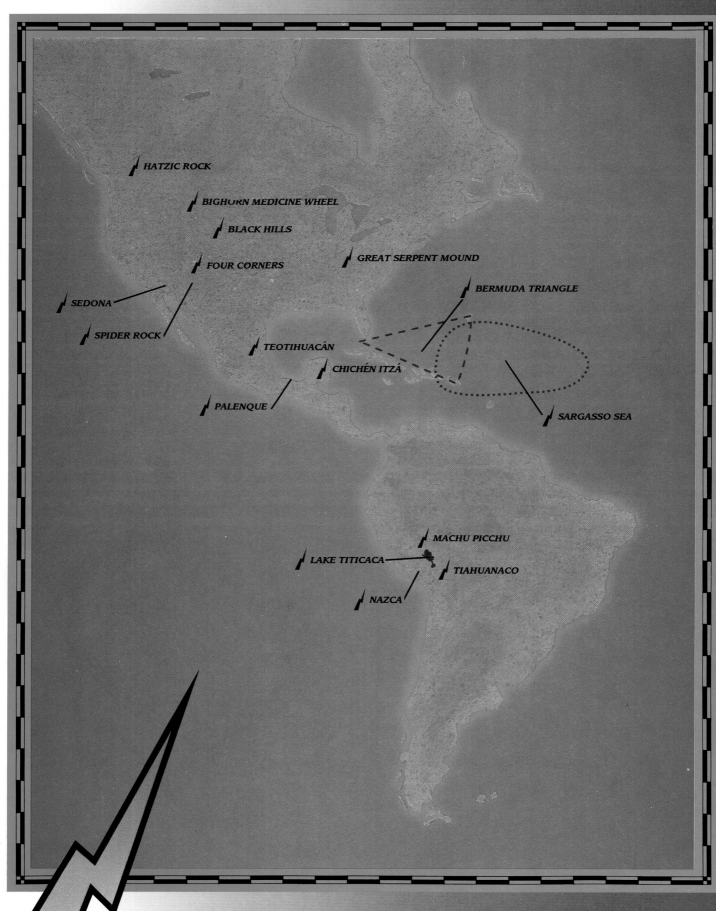

HATZIC ROCK

BIGHORN MEDICINE WHEEL

BLACK HILLS

FOUR CORNERS

GREAT SERPENT MOUND

BERMUDA TRIANGLE

SEDONA

SPIDER ROCK

TEOTIHUACÁN

CHICHÉN ITZÁ

SARGASSO SEA

PALENQUE

MACHU PICCHU

LAKE TITICACA

TIAHUANACO

NAZCA

partly to make clear to vacillating adherents that the take-over was complete and final, but also because the places seemed to possess a transcendent power that the new creed could not ignore. Many Christian churches were thus erected on sites regarded as holy by their previous pagan tenants. Memories of the old religions survived, and these, coupled with the timeless, commonplace human fear of the unknown and fascination with the mysterious, ensure that even today the pyramids of Egypt, the temples of Central America, and the standing stones of western Europe generate awe and inspire stories of extraordinary, sometimes inexplicable goings-on attributable to them.

Such a place is Paha Sapa ("Hills That Are Black"), that part of southwestern South

The Mayan "House of the Ruler" in Mexico's Yucatán

Dakota where grew the spiritual roots of the Crow Indians, then the Ponca, then the Cheyenne, and finally, from the late eighteenth century onward, the Sioux. Here lives the Sioux's Wakan Tanka, the all-encompassing and all-powerful "Great Mystery." And from here, the Sioux believe, through a portal called Wind Cave, the tribe's ancestors first emerged from their subterranean world. In hard times, Sioux shamans, the Wicasa Wakan, retreat to the sanctuary of the Black Hills to commune with the gods and to practice rites that will stave off disaster.

The need for such retreats became more frequent in the late nineteenth century, as the U.S. government reneged on the Treaty of Laramie, signed in 1868, which had officially recognized Sioux control of the Black Hills.

Power Places in the Western Hemisphere

BERMUDA TRIANGLE
The waters north of the Greater Antilles are said to be rife with mysterious forces that cause instrument malfunctions, freak waves, and other effects—sometimes with dire consequences for ships and aircraft.

BIGHORN MEDICINE WHEEL
American Indians say this 800-year-old circle of stones in northern Wyoming has "medicine"—spiritual power. Cairns at its rim align with the sun at the summer solstice and with bright stars on other dates.

BLACK HILLS
Sacred to the Sioux, this mountain range in southwestern South Dakota continues to draw Indians for annual religious rites that include fasting, praying, and vision quests.

CHICHÉN ITZÁ
At this important Mayan religious center on Mexico's Yucatán Peninsula, ritual dancers wore the skins of flayed human sacrificial victims. The skins symbolized transition from death to new life.

FOUR CORNERS
Where Utah, Colorado, Arizona, and New Mexico meet, this point is surrounded by lands sacred to both the Navajo and Hopi nations. It is also frequently mentioned as the site of the Seven Cities of Cibola.

GREAT SERPENT MOUND
Time, it seems, has not robbed this Indian earthwork in southern Ohio of its magic. On a windless day in 1975, leaves at the site reportedly gathered themselves and crept toward a visiting sociologist.

HATZIC ROCK
This tall boulder, located sixty miles east of Vancouver, British Columbia, is believed to hold the spirits of four Indian chiefs who were petrified by the gods for impertinence.

LAKE TITICACA
Situated at 12,500 feet on the Bolivia-Peru border, Titicaca is the world's highest large lake—and is believed to be the spot where the sun god set down his son and daughter, who established the Inca Empire.

MACHU PICCHU
Once home to a thousand Incas, this city in the Peruvian Andes lay unknown to the outside world—thus escaping destruction by the Spanish as a pagan site—from the 1570s until its rediscovery in 1911.

NAZCA
Mysteriously etched onto a desert near Nazca, Peru, before AD 500, the miles-long straight lines, immense animal shapes, and striking geometric patterns here can be made out only from high in the air.

PALENQUE
Carvings on a sarcophagus lid have led some to believe this Mayan ceremonial center in Mexico was built to commemorate an alien visitation. The lid seems to depict an astronaut at the controls of a spaceship.

SARGASSO SEA
Currents are said to have carried wrecked ships from all over the world to this seaweed-clotted mid-Atlantic area. Here they would drift until they sank, their crews dead but denied a peaceful grave.

SEDONA
Visitors often claim to experience strange sensations and take on paranormal abilities while in this part of Arizona. Psychics say the place has four power spots, or vortices, whence the earth emits energy.

SPIDER ROCK
According to Hopi lore, this 800-foot stone spire in Canyon de Chelly, Arizona, is home to the earth goddess Spider Woman. She is said to guard the portal through which humans first emerged.

TEOTIHUACÁN
Already a ruin before the Aztecs found it, this one-time metropolis northeast of today's Mexico City was the work of an unknown people who were masters of architecture, government, and the arts.

TIAHUANACO
Mystery shrouds the ruins of this sophisticated city on a desolate 13,000-foot-high plain near La Paz, Bolivia. Some say it was built by the Egyptians or Phoenicians; some believe the builders came from Atlantis.

In short order the Sioux's powerful position as masters of the northern Great Plains was destroyed. First, the Northern Pacific Railroad pushed deep into their territory. Then an army expedition led by Colonel George Armstrong Custer scouted the Black Hills and returned with confirmation of the old rumors of gold in the hills. A wave of prospectors surged toward this would-be El Dorado, and the government, unable to keep them out, attempted to buy the Black Hills outright from the Sioux, offering a hefty six million dollars.

When the Sioux refused to give up their sacred lands, Custer returned, full of arrogant self-confidence and ambition, and on June 25, 1876, had his fateful rendezvous with several thousand warriors of the Sioux and allied tribes, resulting in the annihilation of his force. Within a year, however, Sioux power was broken by the army, and the nation's survivors were herded into reservations.

Despite the misfortunes and maltreatment they have experienced since that time, the Sioux have never renounced their sacred connection to the Black Hills. Elizabeth Cook, a Sioux and a professor of English/Indian Studies at Eastern Washington University, tells of a trip home she made in a little caravan of cars led by her father. When their route took them to the entrance to Custer State Park in the Black Hills area, a park attendant stopped them to demand the three-dollar entrance fee. Cook's father got out of his car and said with a sweep of his hand, "This is Sioux country. You cannot stop me here in my own land. I am a Dakota and I belong here." With that, the caravan proceeded past the stunned attendant into the park. Neither the decades of gold mining and other sacrileges upon the land nor the high authority of the government could diminish for the Sioux the mystical attraction of the Black Hills.

The Spanish *conquistadores* would have understood the passion for gold that compelled nineteenth-century Americans to violate the sanctity of the Black Hills. More than 300 years earlier, consumed by their own quest for riches, they had shown similar disregard for the places that were held sacred by the native peoples they encountered in the Western Hemisphere.

Ironically, the Spaniards in the Americas had a mystical site of their own to bend the knee to—if only they could find it. This mysterious place was the legendary Seven Cities of Cibola. Rumored to be a realm so rich its streets were paved with silver and gold and its houses inlaid with precious jewels, the Seven Cities had supposedly been founded by a bishop who chose exile and the perils of an unknown ocean rather than stick around while the sword of Islam, wielded by the all-conquering Moors, swept across his native Portugal in the eighth century.

Whether such a bishop indeed came to the New World more than 700 years before Columbus is debatable, but the legend itself certainly took root and grew amid a tangle of Indian traditions. As might have been expected, the Seven Cities were said to lie just over the horizon—due north, in the case of the conquistadors in Mexico.

In 1539 and 1540, two costly and futile expeditions to find the lost cities were dispatched into what is now the American Southwest. The latter party was goaded by deliberate Indian rumors to wander farther and farther in quest of the chimerical Cibola. It reached as far as present-day Kansas before returning empty-handed in 1542.

Had the Spaniards been less obsessed with gold and more accommodating in their encounters with other cultures, they might have appreciated the Southwest for the treasure it was and still is: a land of stark beauty and a place that has been inhabited by spirits as well as humans for at least 6,000 years. Indeed, Francisco Vásquez de Coronado, leader of the second search for the Seven Cities, traveled very near the mythical Four Corners country, where today New Mexico, Arizona, Colorado, and Utah meet. Here, Indians known as the Anasazi had held sway for hundreds of years in their Great Houses—multistoried complexes of tooled masonry—or their magnificent, sprawling cliffside pueblos, until their mysterious disappearance in the thirteenth and fourteenth centuries.

Today, the beliefs and crafts of the Anasazi live on among their presumed descendants, the Hopi, and among an unrelated people, the Navajo—or Diné, as they call themselves. The Hopi live primarily on their Arizona reservation, which is surrounded entirely by the far larger reservation of the Navajo. For the Navajo, the sculptured rock formations, painted desert, and blood-red canyons of the Four Corners country form part of the sacred 25,000-square-mile landscape of Dinetah, "the land of the People."

So many mountains, buttes, mesas, and pueblos are considered dwelling places for the supernatural beings of the Indians' beliefs that this area, comprising the northeast quarter of Arizona and bits of the other Four Corners states, constitutes a vast mystical landscape.

In northwestern New Mexico, for example, east of the Navajo reservation but central to the spiritual life of the Dine, is the Anasazi pueblo of Chaco Canyon. Here, according to Navajo lore, the godlike Holy People showed the first

The ruins of Tiahuanaco (below) stretch across the tree-less plains of Bolivia some 13,000 feet above sea level. In the foreground stands the par-tially restored Kalasasaya, the main temple of the unknown sun worshipers who dwelt at Tiahuanaco in its heyday a millennium ago. The lumpy mound behind the sanctuary is the Akapana, the only visible portion of a step pyramid cam-ouflaged over the centuries by migrating topsoil and tenacious grasses. Tiahuanaco puzzles archaeologists today as it did the Incas many centuries ago. Those first discoverers of the ruins, sensing the mysterious aura of the place, believed that the statues they found there, such as the eleven-and-a-half-foot-tall example at left, were giants who built the city but were later turned into stone by the mighty sun god Viracocha as punishment for misdeeds. A god's face—possibly that of Viracocha—is depicted upon the massive structure known as the Gateway of the Sun (bottom).

Navajo how to organize their society. To the Hopi, too, Chaco Canyon is sacred, a way station on their ancestors' route to their present home. Among Chaco's mysteries is why its residents, who did not possess the wheel, took the trouble to build an estimated 400 miles of roads radiating in all directions.

For the Navajo, the Dinetah is bounded by such sacred peaks as Utah's Navajo Mountain, rainbow hued and, in the words of one modern-day observer, rising "like an apparition from the rose-colored desert . . . the essence of everything reticent, unknowable." For half a millennium the Navajo have looked upon this mountain as a storehouse of energy, a concept that would not be foreign to those New Age mystics who believe in vortices, places from which the earth's stored psychic energy is supposedly emitted.

No list of such energy reservoirs would be complete without the name of one of the world's most publicized places of power, the Bermuda Triangle. The supposed dark forces of this expanse of Atlantic waters off the southeast United States coast have made their greatest impression on the public mind in this century, but one part of the region, the Sargasso Sea, has a much longer recorded history.

The Sargasso Sea, like the New World, was discovered by Christopher Columbus. The "Sea of Fear" and the "Graveyard of Lost Ships" were names given it by later seafarers, many of whom could speak firsthand of this realm of dead water, where masses of seaweed and debris float in the lazily eddying current and where, in the days of sail, a ship might be becalmed for days or weeks on end.

Today, the Sargasso Sea is known among scientists as the breeding ground of the common eel, but it has also bred its share of eerie and fear-inspiring tales. Ships would become entangled in the seaweed, sailors told one another, and once trapped would drift helplessly in a suffocating calm while the crew, half out of their minds, grew weak and died from starvation or thirst, until finally the hull timbers rotted and the vessel sank. The lost spirits of the crew would then join the ranks of the ghosts who were said to haunt this watery graveyard, while beneath them horrifying sea monsters, the mutant offspring of abandoned animals, patrolled the briny depths.

As Columbus also learned during his passage through this weed-choked sea, compass needles no longer pointed toward the North Star. He quickly deduced that his instruments must be pointing toward something else; today, that something else is known to be the north magnetic pole. Far more alarming to the future admiral of the ocean sea was a mysterious glow on the horizon he saw while crossing the Sargasso Sea, a sighting that was confirmed by two members of his crew. To this day, the source of that glow—which quickly came and went as if a candle was being raised and lowered—has never been satisfactorily explained.

This eerie stretch of water was only the first of many mysterious and powerful New World sites that would come to the attention of Europeans over the next few centuries. Another was a spot on the wind-swept high plain of Bolivia. There, not far from La Paz, the cloud-high ruins of the vanished civilization of Tiahuanaco stand silently against the ragged edge of the Andes. So ancient and imposing is the site that even the Incas of the thirteenth century, upon encountering it, were at once baffled and awed.

Unable to explain who had built this extraordinary temple complex and what had become of so sophisticated a people, the Incas spoke instead of Viracocha, the White God, and of a botched attempt at creation. Tiahuanaco, said the Incas, was all that remained of that epic blunder, a city built by giants who had run afoul of Viracocha. For their arrogance, Viracocha turned the delinquent giants to stone—the statues now strewn around the ruins of this city—before wiping the slate clean with a great flood and beginning anew. This time, said the Incas, the White God's creative efforts proved more successful, as he fashioned a race of normal-size human beings, the Incas themselves.

Even today, little is known about the builders of Tiahuanaco, other than what can be seen and what can be deduced by archaeologists: Huge stones, some weighing more than 100 tons, cut without the use of iron or steel tools and precisely fitted to their neighbors without mortar, attest to the skill of the lost city's stonemasons. The ruins of an extensive system of roads and irrigation canals point to the prowess of Tiahuanaco's engineers. A sophisticated drainage and sewage system, together with a handful of gold statues and ornaments salvaged from the ruins, hint at a culture that, in its time, might have been the equal of any civilization in Europe.

All of this was unknown to the Old World when Tiahuanaco was emerging as the preeminent power of central South America in the centuries after AD 600. By 1200, however, the ruins of the temples, fortresses, and step pyramids littered the landscape as they do today. Tiahuanaco was no more, its decline as shrouded in mystery as its shadowy origins.

Perhaps, as some believe, the city was destroyed by a cataclysmic upthrust of the Andes, or perhaps its people were massacred by a neighboring hostile tribe. A more likely scenario is that Tiahuanaco fell victim to a prolonged drought that, in turn, led to the failure of its irrigation sys-

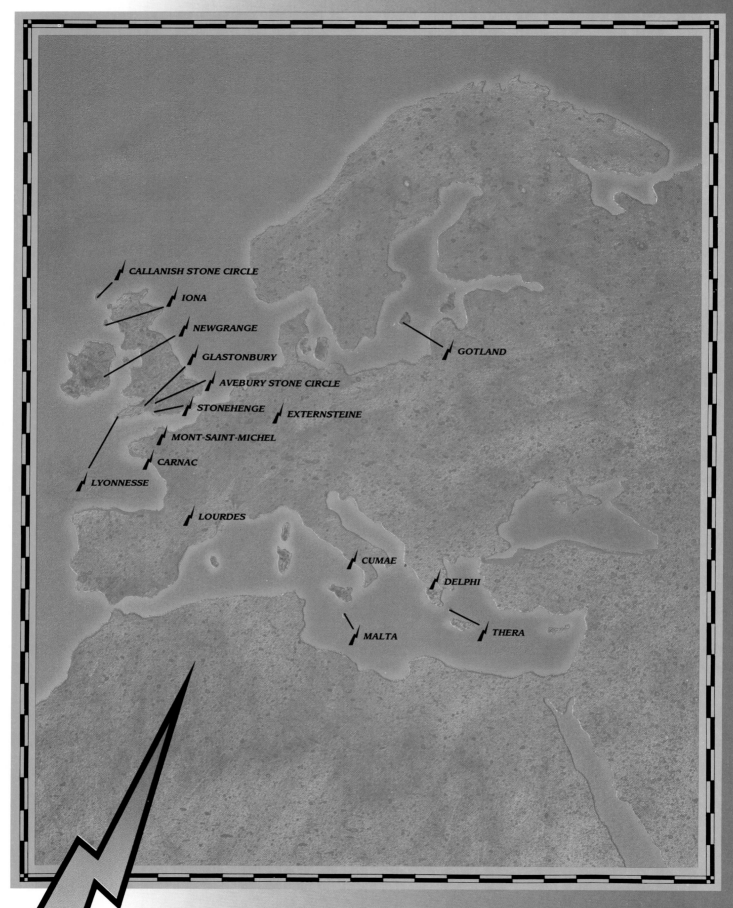

CALLANISH STONE CIRCLE

IONA

NEWGRANGE

GLASTONBURY

AVEBURY STONE CIRCLE

STONEHENGE

EXTERNSTEINE

MONT-SAINT-MICHEL

CARNAC

LYONNESSE

GOTLAND

LOURDES

CUMAE

DELPHI

MALTA

THERA

tem and a return to the barren, dry conditions so apparent nowadays. The truth, whatever it may be, lies locked within the stones of Tiahuanaco, which continue to exert on visitors today the same silent but compelling energy the Incas felt in their presence.

While the Americas' prehistoric cultures were encountering or creating places of power that still endure, the Europeans too were finding meaning and potency in special locations. At about the same time that Tiahuanaco was rising to prominence, an ocean away a monk named Columba was beginning his voluntary exile on Iona, a Scottish isle that would in later centuries become one of Europe's holiest sites.

The year was 563, and Columba, having quarreled with the Irish High King, had left his native Ireland in the

company of twelve followers. Once on Iona, they built a monastery, a crude wattle-and-daub affair, that later became the springboard for the monks' missionary efforts in the rest of Scotland. There, they worked to spread the spirit of the Gospel and, coincidentally, the Irish gift for distilling spirits of the alcoholic sort.

Columba was soon revered as a saint, and for the next two centuries, the abbey he founded at Iona remained the seedbed of the Celtic church. In 795, however, the marauding Vikings paid the island the first of many murderous visits. By 806, after a raid that left the original monastery in ashes and eighty-six monks dead, the survivors pulled up stakes and sailed for safer shores. Repeated attempts to reestablish the monastery were followed by repeated raids, and not until the Norsemen had themselves been converted to Chris-

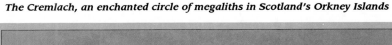
The Cremlach, an enchanted circle of megaliths in Scotland's Orkney Islands

Europe's Points of Energy

AVEBURY STONE CIRCLE
This ring of standing stones in Wiltshire, England—within which lies a whole village—may have been a prehistoric locus of earth energies. Medieval Christians, fearful of its pagan aura, partially dismantled it.

CALLANISH STONE CIRCLE
Legend has it that the tall boulders making up this prehistoric circle on the Isle of Lewis, in Scotland's Outer Hebrides, are actually heathen giants who rejected Christianity and were turned to stone in punishment.

CARNAC
Rows of erect stones near this Breton hamlet may have served as an observatory. The spot may also have been the center of a prehistoric cattle cult, echoed today by an annual blessing of local farmers' cows.

CUMAE
The Sibyl of Cumae described by the poet Virgil delivered her oracles in a cave beneath this Greek colony, twelve miles northwest of Naples, Italy. A Christian church was built on the site in the sixth century.

DELPHI
This sacred site near Mount Parnassus, considered the center of the world by ancient Greeks, is thought to be where Apollo slew the great serpent Pytho and established his famous oracle.

EXTERNSTEINE
First venerated in prehistoric times, these 100-foot-tall stone outcrops near Detmold, Germany, still draw pilgrims of many beliefs. Some say the stones afford access to powerful energies within the earth.

GLASTONBURY
The purported site of the Holy Grail, King Arthur's and Saint Patrick's graves, a gateway to a pagan netherworld, and a zodiac carved into the countryside, this town may be England's premier place of power.

GOTLAND
Mystical sites proliferate on this Swedish island in the Baltic. Bronze Age stone mounds, Iron Age forts, and ship graves— stones set in the outline of ships, to convey souls to the afterlife—dot its landscape.

IONA
Christians of all denominations come to the Inner Hebrides to worship on this sacred isle, home of the Celtic church founded by Saint Columba and reputed burial place of forty-eight Scottish kings.

LOURDES
Each year, millions of pilgrims visit this town in southwestern France to bathe in the waters of a grotto where the Virgin Mary reportedly appeared to a girl in 1858. Thousands of the visitors have claimed miraculous cures.

LYONNESSE
The Seven Stones, exposed bits of rock in the waters between Cornwall's Land's End and the Scilly Isles, are supposedly all that remain of this land whose villages and farms, it is said, were engulfed by the sea.

MALTA
Three Stone Age temples near Valletta, linked with caverns housing statues of an obese woman, suggest a Maltese religion venerating an earth mother. Its adherents had vanished by the Bronze Age.

MONT-SAINT-MICHEL
The church crowning this prominence off Normandy sits on a site used for worship in pre-Christian times. Legend says the archangel Michael ordered the church's construction in the eighth century.

NEWGRANGE
The ancients may have placed their departed in this womblike tomb near Dublin, Ireland, to ensure their rebirth in the afterworld. The structure is aligned to catch a beam of life-giving sunlight at the winter solstice.

STONEHENGE
Even after centuries of study, this ancient circle of massive stones near Salisbury—thought at different times to be an astronomical observatory, a Druid temple, or petrified giants— remains an enigma.

THERA
Scientists believe this tiny island in the Aegean Sea is the remnant of a volcano active in prehistoric times. Its eruption may have devastated the ancient Minoan civilization and inspired the tale of Atlantis.

Legends about the churning seas off Cornwall (right) say a land called Lyonnesse sank from sight there centuries ago. One story has the magician Merlin drowning Lyonnesse by conjuring up an earthquake. Another tells of Trevilian, who fled on a white steed; that horse's likeness still rises from the waves on the Trevellyan family shield (above).

tianity was it finally rebuilt with some expectation that it would remain standing.

Despite Iona's stormy history, its reputation as a singularly holy site flourished, and the island became the burial place of choice for as many as forty-eight Scottish kings, including the ill-fated Duncan, slain by Macbeth in 1040, and, seventeen years later, the wretched Macbeth himself. Not to be left out, more than a dozen foreign kings—from Norway, Ireland, and France—supposedly elected to spend their eternities in the embrace of Iona's sacred soil, which is said to cleanse one of sin.

The Reformation spelled the end of the monks' tenure at Iona in 1561, though the nuns stayed on until the property passed to the McLeans of Duart in 1574; it eventually wound up in the hands of the duke of Argyll in 1693. A little more than 200 years later, in 1899, the eighth duke of Argyll presented the ruins of the twelfth-century abbey, as well as those of a later church and convent and the surrounding grounds, to the Church of Scotland.

But in 1979, six years after the death of the eleventh duke of Argyll, Iona's spiritual mystique was overshadowed for a time by the proposed sale of the island. Unfortunately for his heirs, the duke had died before a time requirement in a tax-saving trust created by his father could be fulfilled, thus leaving his own son, the twelfth duke, liable for some one million pounds in death duties. In an effort to raise the money, the estate's trustees announced that nearly all of Iona was going to be placed on the market. Offers in excess of the proposed one-million-dollar asking price poured in from the United States, Canada, and Australia. A national uproar promptly exploded over the potential loss of the "cradle of Scottish Christianity."

The depth of feeling was apparent in the newspapers of the time. Commenting on the importance of Iona to the people of Scotland and on the vulnerability of a place that is part shrine, part historic site, and part living community, one newspaper intoned, "To walk on Iona is to tread upon the history of Scotland," and cited a visitor to Iona Abbey who remarked that to imperil the peace of such a place would be "a sacrilege." A letter writer to an Edinburgh newspaper was even more to the point: "To allow such places to pass into alien or developing hands would indeed confirm the death of a nation's soul."

The soul of Scotland was secured the day after Iona officially went on the block, when a private foundation bought the island and subsequently conveyed it into the sure, safe hands of the National Trust for Scotland.

Less fortunate and forever lost, if tradition is true, was

a fertile and once-prosperous fragment of Celtic Cornwall that vanished, some say, under a torrent of seawater. This disaster is said to have occurred sometime around AD 500. Numerous villages and farms and an entire city all slipped beneath the waves, according to legend, leaving only one man to tell the tale. That man, named Trevilian, escaped to the Cornish mainland on a white charger, galloping at breakneck speed as the sea closed in behind him. To this day the family, its name now spelled Trevellyan, uses a crest bearing the image of a white horse.

Lyonnesse, as this legendary land was known, supposedly linked Land's End, at the extreme southwestern tip of England, and Saint Michael's Mount, a short way up the Cornish coast, with the Scilly Isles, located some twenty-five miles offshore. "The lost land of Lyonnesse," as the poet Alfred, Lord Tennyson called it, also figures in the legends of King Arthur, specifically as the home of Tristan, the noblest of Arthur's knights and the doomed lover of the fair Isolde. Tennyson himself, in his *Idylls of the King,* exercised poetic license and made Lyonnesse the site of his "many-towered Camelot" and the setting for Arthur's final battle. The return of Arthur, say staunch believers in the story, will be heralded by the sight of drowned Lyonnesse rising from the waves.

Apart from legend and the reports of early chroniclers, the facts are few that would substantiate such a once and future kingdom. Even so, the fossilized remains of a forest can be seen at low tide in the waters surrounding the small island of Saint Michael's Mount. Moreover, on the submerged salt flats that separate the Scilly Isles there is some evidence of one-time human habitation—lines of stones that may have been walls separating tilled fields. Most tantalizing of all is the report of a church bell tolling mournfully from beneath the waves that cover vanished Lyonnesse.

The story of Lyonnesse echoes similar tales told of the drowned city of Ys, or Ker-Is, which reportedly lay off the coast of Brittany in northern France. Lending credence to this Breton story, however, is the fact that the nearly land-locked Gulf of Morbihan, on the south coast of the Breton Peninsula south of Vannes, was actually formed sometime after neolithic times when the land settled and was engulfed by the Atlantic Ocean. Even today, the tips of submerged megalithic monuments can be seen off the coast when the tide is out.

The megaliths themselves were part of an extensive complex of stone monuments, or menhirs, that pepper the Breton Peninsula, with some 3,000 of them concentrated in

This massive stone is just one of 982 that make up the Kermario Alignment, a so-called place of the dead, amid the awe-inspiring forest of prehistoric megaliths erected around the present-day village of Carnac, France. French noble and antiquary the Chevalier de Fréminville sketched what he designated the "funereal monuments" in the 1824 map below.

the area around the tiny village of Carnac. There are four groups of the stones in all, one of which, the Kermario, or "the place of the dead," stretches 4,000 feet in ten rows. Nearby is the tomb of Kercado, itself surrounded by a circle of standing stones posted like sentinels. Another stone guards the grass-covered mound of the tomb, whose entrance opens almost exactly on the midwinter sunrise. Carbon-dated to 4700 BC, Kercado is the oldest structure in all of Europe, older than the Knossos palaces of Crete and older by 2,000 years than Stonehenge.

Not far away is Le Grand Menhir Brisé, or, as it is also known, Er Grah, "The Fairy Stone," which, the archaeological evidence suggests, may have been used by neolithic peoples as a giant marker for tracking the movements of the moon. The largest monolith ever set upright, it measured more than sixty feet in height and weighed about 340 tons in its unbroken state. Toppled by an earthquake in 1722, it lies today in four enormous pieces. Prehistoric astronomers would sight through Le Grand Menhir from smaller menhirs as far as nine miles away.

Although the Carnac megaliths were set in place at various times between 4700 and 2000 BC, well before Roman legionnaires trod this land as conquerors, the local peasants still think of the stones as "petrified soldiers." They hark back to a legend that recounts how Roman soldiers once chased the early Christian saint and pope Cornély all the way to Brittany from Rome. Trapped at the edge of the sea, Cornély spun around and, much to the surprise of his pursuers, blessed them. Presumably, these fanciful centurions were even more surprised to find themselves suddenly transformed into stone.

Seen from above, their ranks stretching into the distance, Carnac's megaliths do bear a striking resemblance to soldiers poised forever in formation. The French antiquary the Chevalier de Fréminville admitted as much in 1827 when he described the megaliths as a "regiment of stones" and recounted how the sight of the stones and the stillness of their setting "astound the imagination and fill the soul

with a melancholy veneration for these ancient witnesses to so many centuries."

For most of those centuries—even in the Roman and early Christian eras—the megaliths were indeed the object of veneration by Bretons, a people with a Celtic appreciation for rocks as receptacles of power. Tilted upright and arranged into stone avenues, sometimes in precise orientation to the sun, the moon, or certain stars, the megaliths became centers of spiritual activity.

They may also have functioned, as some believe, as conduits of the earth's vital energy, revivifying the surrounding soil and increasing its fertility. Such energy, unseen and yet perceptible, is said to emanate from one of Germany's most sacred places, the Externsteine, five 120-foot-high sandstone pillars extruded from the ancient floor of the Teutoburg Forest in the western part of the country, near Osnabrück. Dowsers working the area claim to have tapped into this power, and dowsers and nondowsers alike profess to have been cured of various ailments while under the influence of the mysterious rock formation. For some, a visit to the Externsteine is tantamount to renewing one's lease on life; one woman returns annually to recline in an ancient stone coffin, convinced that only this annual ritual is keeping her among the living.

Altogether, as many as 800,000 people visit the Externsteine each year. For the most part they come to be bewitched by the natural beauty and drama of the site and to clamber up the rock-hewn parapets and ramble through the warren of caves and grottoes. But the pillars' powerfully mystical aura also attracts members of various fringe movements, who tend to invest the place with powers in accordance with their own dogmas and passions.

Today's visitors are only the most recent in a long line of pilgrims who have been coming to the Externsteine since prehistoric times. In those dim days of yore, the rocks were a ritual center for neolithic Germany's nomadic reindeer hunters. Later, the Externsteine became a holy site for more sedentary pagans and remained that way until late in the eighth century AD, when Charlemagne outlawed heathen

Sandstone outcrops known as the Externsteine (above) rise beside a lake in north-central Germany. An ancient cult of light worshipers began the practice of hewing chambers out of the rocks and performing rituals there. They reportedly greeted the summer sun as it cast its rays through the circular window at right and may have initiated novices in the coffinlike niche carved in the rock at left, which even today is accorded special powers.

worship there. Christian monks moved in, settling into the chambers and niches that had been so conveniently gouged out by the previous tenants and adapting the place to suit their own needs. Lest anyone doubt that the Externsteine were under new management, a later generation of monks killed two birds with one stone, so to speak, by adorning one rock face with a bas-relief carving that depicts Christ's removal from the cross and symbolizes the triumph of Christianity over paganism.

In what some might see as both the return and the revenge of paganism, the Externsteine attracted the attention of the Nazis and specifically of SS commandant Heinrich Himmler, who made the rocky spires the backdrop for secret SS rituals. The site was convenient to Wewelsburg, the seventeenth-century fortress that Himmler and his henchmen transformed into a Nazi Camelot, complete with a round table and a "holy of holies," where the ashes of fallen SS heroes were entombed.

Fueling Nazi interest in the Externsteine, apart from their location and their longstanding reputation as a kind of German Stonehenge, was their role in a theory put forward by Wilhelm Teudt, a German evangelical parson, in the 1920s. Teudt asserted that the Externsteine and other sites in the Teutoburg Forest were the heart of a system of straight pathways called *heilige Linien*, or holy lines. He also said that these lines formed an invisible chain linking a more-than-coincidental number of standing stones, churches, towers, and crosses, much as so-called ley lines are said to do in England.

Teudt also maintained that the roofless Christian chapel long ago carved from the rock of the Externsteine's tallest spire was neither Christian nor a chapel, but an ancient observatory dating back to pagan times. A circular window in one wall of the chamber is precisely sited for viewing the sunrise at the midsummer solstice and for observing the moon when it rises to its most northerly position. Curiously, too, the Externsteine share virtually the same latitude with another alleged observatory, Stonehenge, a fact that has not gone unnoticed by those who believe that pre-Christian Europe was once the domain of an enlightened order of astronomer-priests.

In service to a priesthood of another kind, another rocky outcrop, this one overlooking Italy's cerulean Bay of Naples, formed the foundation for a pair of temples, one dedicated to Jupiter, the other to Apollo. Lower on the cliff face lay a cave that, beginning as early as the sixth or fifth century BC, was venerated by the Greeks as the home of the Sibyl of Cumae.

The Cumaean sibyl was the most famous of all the sibyls serving as oracles for the god Apollo by divining the future on his behalf. Pilgrims who came to consult the oracle would enter the cave and pass down a 300-foot-long corridor lit from the sides by twelve intersecting galleries that functioned as light wells. The effect of walking through alternating pools of light and shadow could only have heightened the anticipation of the sibyl's visitors as they made their way toward the vestibule at the end of the corridor and stepped into a vaulted chamber to receive her prophecies. Once there, cowering in the half-light, they might have heard, as Virgil says Aeneas and his Trojans heard, "horrible enigmas and growls from the chamber, enveloping the truth in the shadows. . . ."

Caves like the one at Cumae had obvious appeal to those who had inherited an understanding of caves as symbols of creation and as transit points between our world and the realm of the spirits. Throughout the ancient world,

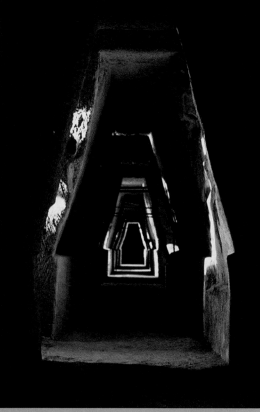

Cut into the flank of a volcanic cliff on Italy's Tyrrhenian coast nearly 3,000 years ago, the cave opening at far left led to the den of the Sibyl of Cumae (above), a fabled prophet. Those seeking her counsel would approach her quarters by walking down a long, eerily lit gallery (near left) that has lost none of its power to infuse visitors with awe.

A former site of Celtic sun worship, France's Mont-Saint-Michel now draws Christian pilgrims.

numerous other oracles set up shop in caves, some of which were then further hollowed out to enhance the drama of the divinations.

Such was the case with the Hypogeum, on the island of Malta. Here, in the fourth millennium BC, workers armed with only the most primitive tools spent centuries scraping and chiseling away at bedrock of solid limestone to carve out an underground complex of chambers, passages, and stairways. Once the Hypogeum was completed, those seeking the counsel of the oracle would huddle in the eerie darkness and listen while the oracle's "voice" rumbled Oz-like from wall to wall, the result of an echo-enhancing ridge purposely carved into the ceiling. This remarkable echo chamber did double duty as a tomb for as many as 6,000 people, before being abandoned around 2500 BC. Not until 1902, when construction workers accidentally breached the roof of the sunken chamber while building a housing development, was the Hypogeum rediscovered.

Most early peoples, however, were not so inclined as the Maltese toward backbreaking subterranean labors. They looked instead for caves that were naturally suited to their purposes. In some instances these caves became the setting for rituals whose original purpose is no longer readily apparent. The walls of the Gargas cave in the French Pyrenees, for example, are covered with more than 150 ghostly hand prints or outlines of hands, painted or stenciled some 35,000 years ago as the Ice Age was drawing to a close. Adding to the intrigue is the fact that nearly all of the hand prints are missing parts of their fingers, the grisly result, perhaps, of some kind of ritual mutilation, performed either to appease the hunting gods or to invoke good luck upon a newborn child.

This human fascination with caves and their symbolism was so deeply ingrained that even the arrival of Christianity did little to dampen their appeal. On the contrary, the new powers-that-be soon set about building up their own inventory of sacred caves, with the grotto at Lourdes, reportedly the site of a vision of the Blessed Mother, being one of the more recent entries on the list. In other cases, the Church claimed old pagan caves for its own, as it did a cave on Italy's Mount Tancia. Once the headquarters of a pagan oracle, it became the object of Christian veneration late in the fifth century after the archangel Michael supposedly appeared there.

As one of the most important Christian saints, celebrated both as the leader of the heavenly host and for his role in the defeat of Satan and the rebel angels, Saint Michael was repeatedly called upon to lend his good name

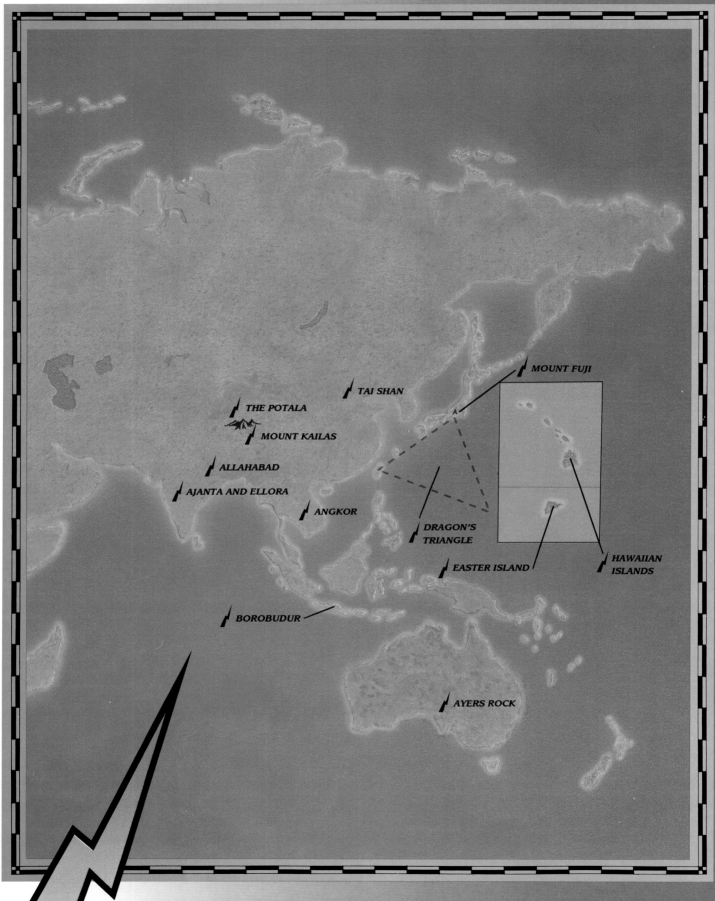

THE POTALA

TAI SHAN

MOUNT KAILAS

ALLAHABAD

AJANTA AND ELLORA

ANGKOR

MOUNT FUJI

DRAGON'S
TRIANGLE

EASTER ISLAND

HAWAIIAN
ISLANDS

BOROBUDUR

AYERS ROCK

to what had formerly been a pagan place of worship or burial—hence the reason why many a church built on a hilltop or a pre-Christian mound or barrow bears the name of Saint Michael.

With its record of organized civilizations dating back as much as four millennia, Asia is dotted with places of power whose authenticity is vouched for by their longevity. One such site is the 5,000-foot-high Tai Shan, the most revered of China's holy mountains and a place of pilgrimage ever since the emperor Shun made the trek to the top around 2200 BC and proclaimed himself the Son of Heaven.

During the middle of the Han dynasty, while the West was making the transition to the Christian era, Tai Shan became more closely associated with the evolving religious and philosophical discipline known as Taoism. Though the mountain had long been venerated as the origin of all life on earth, it was now imagined as the seat of an otherworldly tribu-

nal that met to pass judgment on the newly dead. Like any tribunal, no matter how otherworldly, this one was not above the occasional error; Chinese legend is rife with stories of those unfortunate souls who were accidentally summoned too soon to the mountain and were generously allowed to return to life.

The pious preferred not to wait until after death for a glimpse of the holy mountain, however, and in the days before China's Communist government cast its baleful frown on such displays of religious devotion, as many as 10,000 pilgrims a day made the day-long climb to the top. The construction centuries ago of 6,700 steps, leading from the walled city of Taian at the mountain's foot all the way to the Temple of the Jade Emperor at its peak, eased the rugged ascent of the Pan Lu, or Pilgrim Way, and created, in effect, a stone-paved stairway to heaven. The more affluent of the pilgrims made the ascent in comfort, riding in shaded bamboo chairs resting on the shoulders of bearers. Some of

Gateway to the long-venerated Temple of Confucius in Tsinghai

Power Centers in Asia and the Pacific

AJANTA AND ELLORA
The temples and chambers at these sites in south-central India, many hewn from single huge stones, are thought to be products of a millennium's work by tens of thousands of Buddhists and Hindus.

ALLAHABAD
Seeking to be freed from repeated reincarnation, Hindus gather in this city every twelve years to crowd into the waters where the Ganges and Yamuna rivers meet—one of India's most powerful sacred spots.

ANGKOR
According to legend, this center of Cambodian Hinduism—the world's largest city in AD 1000—was abandoned after the snake god, enraged by the murder of a priest's son, caused a devastating flood.

AYERS ROCK
Though the face of this massive rock in central Australia is continuously being altered by erosion, the Aborigine people hold its surface features to be the marks of their giant, semidivine ancestors.

BOROBUDUR
Considered a three-dimensional model of the Buddhist cosmos, this ornate temple on Java is believed to offer spiritual enlightenment to pilgrims who climb clockwise around its six concentric levels.

DRAGON'S TRIANGLE
Like the Bermuda Triangle, this area between Yap Island, Taiwan, and Japan is a source of baffling phenomena, including the "triangle wave," which is said to hit ships from three directions simultaneously.

EASTER ISLAND
Hundreds of stone figures with huge human heads glare across this tiny isle in the South Pacific. They stand on platforms on which the islanders consigned their dead to the elements.

HAWAIIAN ISLANDS
Throughout Hawaii are prehistoric engineering works allegedly built by the menehune, a legendary race of dwarfish humanoids. Some believe the menehune are as real as the projects attributed to them.

MOUNT FUJI
This highest of Japanese peaks is sacred to Buddhists, for whom it is a gateway to another world, and to Shintoists, who have built numerous shrines dedicated to Sengen-Sama, the mountain's goddess.

MOUNT KAILAS
Although exceedingly rugged and remote, this mountain in Tibet has been the destination of pilgrims for more than a thousand years. They consider it the center of the world, a dwelling place of gods.

THE POTALA
According to popular belief, this golden-roofed former palace of the Dalai Lamas in Lhasa, Tibet, is the handiwork of the gods, who are said to have raised it in a single night.

TAI SHAN
This majestic mountain in eastern China was venerated by Chinese emperors for about 4,000 years—even though for most of that time it was sacred to Taoism and not to the state religion, Confucianism.

the especially devout, on the other hand, not only went on foot but would kowtow every few steps the whole way up.

Over the centuries the mountain has become encrusted with shrines and temples, many of them strung along the Pan Lu. At each of these stops, pilgrims could offer prayers to a particular deity, some of whom are thought to control humanity's fate on earth. They could even pray to Tai Shan itself, since the mountain is considered a god in its own right and one well worth supplication.

The path also winds past such descriptively named milestones as the Tower of Ten Thousand Fairies, the Peach Orchard Glen, and the Snowflake Bridge. Nearer the top, the passageway called the Dragon's Throat waits to swallow approaching worshipers, funneling them up the Slow Eighteen Flights and then up the thousand steep steps of the Sudden Eighteen Flights toward the stone portal of the South Heavenly Gate. Beyond this gate lies the Heavenly Way; beyond it, the Temple of the Jade Emperor.

Not far from the temple stands the Tablet Without Inscription, a stone monument some fifteen feet high, four feet wide, and three feet thick, quarried elsewhere and transported here more than 2,000 years ago by means of exertions difficult to imagine. Tradition has it that a poet was led to this spot and asked to sing the praises of the mountain on the blank tablet. Dumbstruck by the splendor of Tai Shan, with all of China spread at his feet, the poet could only manage the single word that appears on the slab today: *Ti,* "the Lord on High."

If legend has served to heighten the attraction of China's most mystical mountain, it has also helped to deepen the mystery surrounding an expanse of water called the Philippine Sea off China's eastern coast. Within this area, say the ancient tales, dragons dwell in undersea palaces, their movements churning up waves even on windless days. Sailors claim to have heard strange noises here, while at night, eerie red lights as bright as the sun could be seen shining over the water from hundreds of miles away.

Tradition has it that the dragons who inhabit these waters, known to the Chinese by the ancient name of the Western Sea, are capricious creatures that, when angry, stir up storms. Most powerful of all is Li-Lung, the dragon king of the Western Sea, whose underwater palace is splendidly furnished with treasures from sunken ships.

It is said that the dragons occasionally rise from their underwater lairs to pluck passing ships from the surface, hauling them to their doom and plundering them of their cargoes. Perhaps because of the alarmingly high number of mysterious sinkings that actually happen within the area—a region roughly triangular in shape with its corners formed by Japan to the north, Yap Island to the south, and Taiwan to the west—this patch of the Pacific has become known as the Dragon's Triangle.

So notorious is the triangle among fishermen that for more than a thousand years the Japanese called it Ma-no Umi, the "Sea of the Devil." Sailors traversing it today have noted a greater-than-normal incidence of compass deviations and breakdowns in radio communications. More ominous still are the unexpected seaquakes, whirlpools, and localized hurricanes that seem to strike more frequently here than in other parts of the Pacific, as well as enormous waves and thick fogs that roll across the open water, engulfing seafarers with awful suddenness.

Because a number of ships vanished inexplicably off Japan's eastern coast during the late 1940s, the Japanese government in 1950 was forced to declare the Izu-shichitō and Bonin island chains a danger zone for shipping. Two years later, in an effort to get to the bottom of the mystery, the government ordered a research vessel, the *Kaiō Maru No. 5,* into the area. On September 24, 1952, while sailing in good weather on calm seas, the *Kaiō Maru No. 5* disappeared without a trace, carrying twenty-two crew members and nine scientists to a rendezvous with the dragon.

The Dragon's Triangle has logged a growing number of victims in the decades since. Numerous reasons have been advanced to account for the disappearances, ranging from a disturbance in the earth's magnetic field to eruptions of undersea volcanoes to what the Japanese call *mikakunin hiko-buttai,* or UFOs. But as there are no survivors to tell tales and no identifiable wreckage to examine, the Dragon's Triangle must remain as unfathomable as its equally notorious Atlantic counterpart, the Bermuda Triangle.

To the south of those seas where dragons dwell in sunken palaces, the Aborigines of Australia long ago peopled their land with beings even more fantastic. They tell of a far-off and dreamy past when the earth was still unformed and a race of Sky Heroes arose to create it and give it life. Adrift in this Dreamtime, or the Dreaming, as the Aborigines call

their mythical age, these supernatural beings wandered at will, and as they wandered they gave shape to the earth. Footprints were transformed into caves, campfires into rock holes, the bodies of fallen giants into boulders. Even the events of the Sky Heroes' everyday lives—births, battles, or the trails left by a tribe as it passed through the countryside—were supposedly written on the landscape.

According to their stories, the Aborigines are themselves the descendants of the Sky Heroes, and those places where the Dreamtime beings or their deeds became physical landmarks were later held sacred. Likewise, myths associated with those places became the spiritual heritage of every Aborigine, a legacy to be cherished and passed on to the next generation.

A tangible symbol of that time beyond time can be found in the hulking mass of Ayers Rock, a gigantic chunk of sandstone that rises 1,143 feet above the flat floor of the vast Australian outback even though fully two-thirds of its enormous bulk is concealed beneath the sands. Named for a nineteenth-century South Australian premier, the rock is found on the southwestern reaches of Australia's Northern Territory, floating iceberglike on the sea of

Amid numbers of tourists, a few Taoist and Buddhist faithful climb the final steps of a seven-hour ascent to the top of the hallowed Chinese mountain Tai Shan, as their ancestors did 4,000 years ago. Some pilgrims begin the grueling journey at nightfall to arrive in time to view the sunrise from the peak.

the surrounding desert, its sheer sides a canvas painted fiery red by the rising or retreating sun.

To the Aborigines, Ayers Rock is Uluru, a place sacred since the Dreamtime and the crossroads of a number of Dreamtime trails, those tracks left by the wandering Sky Heroes. Here, in the Dreaming, lived such mythical tribes as the Hare Wallaby people, the Venomous Snake people, and the Carpet Snake people. And here, etched in the rock's weathered surface, is their legendary history. Boulders on the sloping southeast side of Ayers Rock are to the Aborigines the body of a Carpet Snake woman; potholes in a cliff face are marks left by Venomous Snake spears; eroded gullies on the wall of a cave are the breasts of nursing Hare Wallaby women. Besides the natural features, petroglyphs chipped into the rock were, according to the Aborigines, the work not of mere mortals but of the Sky Heroes.

Uluru also tells of the clashes between these various tribes and of their encounters with such totemic creatures as the Sleepy-lizard man, the Willy Wagtail woman, and the Devil Dingo. In one of the more famous battles immortalized on Ayers Rock, the leader of the Venomous Snake people fought a warrior of the Carpet Snakes at Mutitjilda, site of a water hole known to outsiders as Maggie Springs. The course of the battle can be traced in cracks in the rock, said to be cuts made by the stone knives of the combatants. Nearby is the trail supposedly left by the wounded Carpet Snake warrior as he crawled toward the spring, while the spring itself is believed to be the man's transformed blood.

Many of Uluru's landmarks are considered so sacred that they are fenced off to bar the entrance of outsiders, a prohibition actively enforced by the Australian government. Even Aborigines not yet initiated or, sometimes, those of one gender or the other are also forbidden entry to particular areas. The women's fertility cave, for example, is off-limits to men. Other places are the private enclaves of men, so taboo that passing women may not even glance in their direction. Within one male redoubt, the Mala cave, renowned among Aborigines as a ''plenteous happy place,'' boys are ritually initiated into the Hare Wallaby tribe.

Hawaiians, too, have a legendary people in their past—but there is lively disagreement among present-day Hawaiians over whether the *menehune* are mythical or real. Allegedly Hawaii's original inhabitants, they are said by some to be an unusual race of beings with supernatural abilities. Others contend that the menehune were at some point in the distant past an ordinary and mortal people who were only elevated to godlike status in the imaginations of later generations of Hawaiians.

Whatever the case, the menehune are described as

two or three feet tall, thickset, and hairy. Moreover, unlike Australia's spiritual forebears, who shaped the land as much by accident as by design, the menehune took a more deliberate approach, using their considerable engineering skill—especially as stonemasons—to build dams, fishponds, watercourses, causeways, and small temples called *heiaus*. And just as some Hawaiians see the menehune as supernatural, to these believers the menehune construction projects, all of them unarguably real, are by definition infused with supernatural power.

Examples of purported menehune-built structures can be found on many of the Hawaiian Islands. Both Kauai and Molokai have fishponds that are said to be of menehune construction, and there are dozens of heiaus scattered throughout the islands that are attributed to the menehune.

The most celebrated of all menehune projects, however, is the Kiki-a-Ola, the so-called Menehune Ditch, on the island of Kauai. Set at the edge of a rain forest, the ditch channels the Waimea River from a hole in a mountainside down around the corner of the mountain. The quality of the stonework commands attention, for although only a small portion of the original ditch remains, the existing stones of the apparently ancient structure are precisely cut and expertly fitted one to another. Such dressed stonework is rare in the Hawaiian Islands, rare enough that many believe that the ditch could only have been built by the menehune.

Few claim to have actually seen the menehune, at least in modern times. Not that Hawaii's playful little people make it easy to spot them; they are said to work only at night, partly out of an aversion to daylight and partly to avoid detection. In fact, any project undertaken by the menehune supposedly must be completed in a single night; if not, the job is abandoned, unfinished, at dawn. Such was the case, apparently, at Kohala on the island of Hawaii, where a watercourse similar to the Menehune Ditch was reportedly hastily abandoned when a cock crowed as daylight suddenly broke.

Nevertheless, in what was the last reported sighting of the menehune, sometime in the late 1940s, forty-five schoolchildren and their school's superintendent claimed to have caught a glimpse of off-duty menehune engineers playing on the lawn across the street from the school. As soon as they realized they were being watched, the little people dived for cover, supposedly slipping under a house and into a tunnel that is said to lead into the mountains.

According to tradition, at some unspecified time in Hawaii's past there were more than half a million menehune on the island of Kauai alone. But the menehune king became alarmed for their future because so many of his

Ayers Rock (above) and Mount Olga, its sister outcrop on the horizon, dominate the scrubby desert of Australia's Northern Territory. An explorer who visited the red sandstone monoliths wrote in 1874, "Mount Olga is the more wonderful and grotesque; Mount Ayers the more ancient and sublime." The latter sentiment is true to the thinking of local Aborigines, who revere Ayers Rock as the dwelling place of the spirits of their creators. These gods are said to have engraved the rock's caves with carvings such as the tree designs at left.

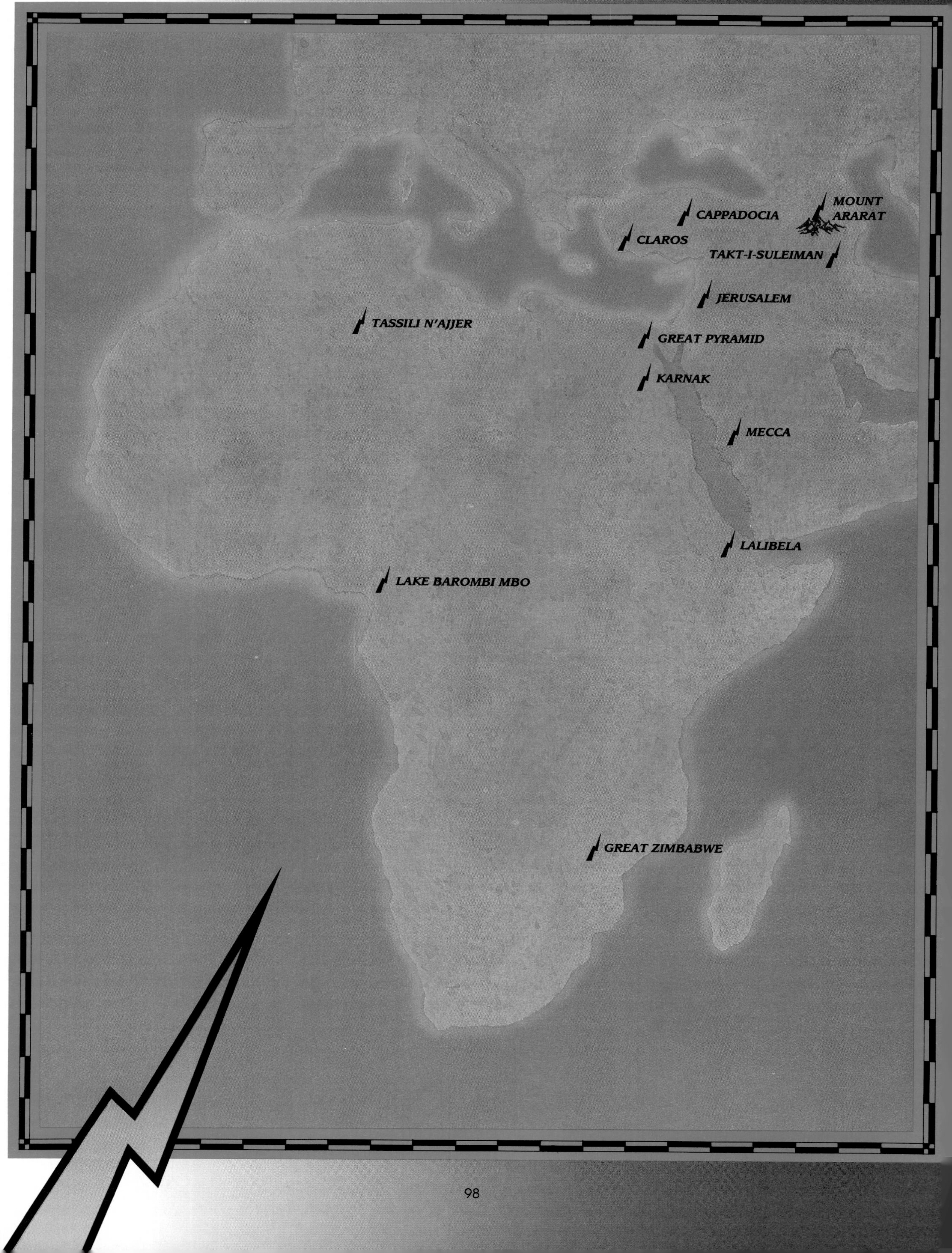

CAPPADOCIA

CLAROS

MOUNT ARARAT

TAKT-I-SULEIMAN

JERUSALEM

TASSILI N'AJJER

GREAT PYRAMID

KARNAK

MECCA

LALIBELA

LAKE BAROMBI MBO

GREAT ZIMBABWE

men were marrying Hawaiian women. Desperate to put an end to the practice, he led an exodus from the island.

Even the legends do not say where the menehune went. But if the results of an early nineteenth-century census are any indication, a few must have chosen to defy the king's wishes and remain behind. That census, done at the request of Kauai's last independent ruler, Kaumualii, counted 2,000 people in the island's Wainiha Valley. Sixty-five of them, the king's agent noted, were menehune.

Another land almost as green and lush as Hawaii also had its places of power, but by the time the modern world discovered them, that teeming grassland had become the Sahara. It is difficult to imagine a time when so empty and arid a place might have been rich and fertile, let alone carved by rippling rivers into plateaus and valleys carpeted with trees and grasses. But 8,000 years ago today's ocean of sand was indeed a well-watered and hospitable land.

Here hunters pursued abundant game, cattle grazed in luxuriant pastures, and civ-

Symbols of mystical energy, the pyramids at Giza, Egypt

ilization took root and flowered. For the next 2,000 years, some scientists speculate, the Sahara may have been the most densely populated region on earth; anthropologists call it a "nursery" for many cultures that spread to other parts of Africa.

All of this began to change, however, when a shift in weather patterns, coupled with the effects of overgrazing, started the process that transformed this verdant land into the scorched and undulating desert whose Arabic name means "the waste." Yet, ironically, the same climatic changes that drove the population from the expanding desert also had the effect of preserving a portrait of its vanished way of life—rendered on the rock walls of one of Africa's most haunting places, Tassili n'Ajjer, the "Plateau of the Rivers," in what is now southeastern Algeria.

There are no rivers at Tassili n'Ajjer today, but the plateau is still there, its cliffs and caves covered with some 15,000 rock paintings and engravings. For more than five millennia this veritable museum of prehistoric African art remained hidden at the dry

Power Places of Africa and the Middle East

CAPPADOCIA
Pagans in this part of central Turkey lived and worshiped in chambers cut from volcanic rock long before Greek Christians arrived in the fourth century and converted the grottoes into churches.

CLAROS
Allegedly a place of divine prophecy, this site in western Turkey drew visitors from all over the known world during the Roman era and was one of the last oracles still operating in Christian times.

GREAT PYRAMID
Dead animals found in this 4,400-year-old wonder, ten miles west of Cairo, offer evidence of the strange effect it is said to have on material things: Though dehydrated, the animals resist decomposition.

GREAT ZIMBABWE
Perhaps showing the prehistoric residents' mystical attachment to the soil, a thirty-foot-tall stone tower at this site south of the Zambezi River may have been a phallic symbol used in crop fertility rituals.

JERUSALEM
For centuries the object of both pilgrims and invading armies, this ancient city is revered by Jews, Muslims, and Christians alike. All three faiths consider it the site of miracles past and future.

KARNAK
Evidence exists that this site south of Cairo was considered sacred centuries before the Egyptians built the prehistoric complex of temples and other structures whose ruins stand here today.

LAKE BAROMBI MBO
Believed to contain a powerful spirit named Mammy Water, this lake in Cameroon is the site of animal sacrifices intended to prevent such troubles as the spread of lethal lake-water gases along the shores.

LALIBELA
Christians living near this town in northern Ethiopia have worshiped for centuries in eleven churches that were painstakingly hewn from solid rock. According to legend, the carvers were assisted by angels.

MECCA
This city in Saudi Arabia, the place toward which Muslims face when praying, surrounds a sacred stone said to have fallen from heaven. Muslims believe the stone was white and turned black absorbing human sin.

MOUNT ARARAT
For years, a dragon, frigid snow worms, and other mythical creatures were thought to guard this 17,000-foot mountain in eastern Turkey. It is believed to be the final resting spot of Noah's Ark.

TAKT-I-SULEIMAN
Sacred to pagans, then Zoroastrians, then Muslims, but never to Christians, this complex on the shores of a supposedly bottomless lake in Iran was nonetheless rumored to be the hiding place of the Holy Grail.

TASSILI N'AJJER
Prehistoric paintings, some almost 7,000 years old, cover this rocky plateau 900 miles southeast of Algiers. Scholars say they hint at mystical practices once common but now lost in the mists of time.

heart of the Sahara, abandoned by those who created it and then largely forgotten.

Not until 1933 did the dazzling art collection come to light again, and then only by accident. A French colonial army Camel Corps patrol wandered into a canyon called Oued Djerat and suddenly found itself surrounded by herds of enormous elephants, rhinoceroses, and giraffes—animals that, for all anyone knew, could not possibly have lived in this sere, sun-blasted part of Africa. All were carved or painted on the rock walls of the enclosing gorge.

A young ethnologist named Henri Lhote, who investigated the new discovery, managed to organize and fund a full-scale examination of the site only after a twenty-three-year delay, including the intervention of World War II. What emerged in that 1956 expedition, as the rock walls slowly yielded their secrets, was a tantalizing glimpse of the region's lost past, captured in scenes that portray the everyday life of prehistoric Africa—the age-old thrill of the hunt, the drama of warfare between neighboring peoples, tranquil moments of music and dance.

Also depicted are scenes of more mystical significance, including some suggesting that for countless years Tassili n'Ajjer may have been the center of religious practices now lost in the mists of time. Some paintings, for example, show what may be initiation rites and ritual sacrifices. Others offer evidence of a fertility cult. Still more depict gods and goddesses, among them an eighteen-foot-high painting of a deity whose size and whose resemblance to newspaper and movie conceptions of space aliens led the artists in Lhote's party to dub it the Great Martian God.

An Egyptian touch can be seen in some of the rock paintings at Tassili n'Ajjer. Some seem to depict sights that were seen by the artists while they were visiting Egypt; others betray the imprint of Egyptian culture on the customs of the Sahara. Moreover, at least one picture appears to portray religious themes that were typical of Egypt—specifically, the voyage of the dead to the afterworld.

That Egypt's influence should be felt so far away from its seat of power at Thebes is not surprising, given the king-dom's status as one of the superpowers of its day. Thebes reigned as the capital of the realm throughout much of the thousand-year run of the Middle and New Kingdoms. And tucked into the northern half of the capital was the temple complex of Karnak, Egypt's great religious center and home base for the cult of Amen, the "king of the gods." Here the Egyptians built and rebuilt the Great Temple of Amen, creating in the end not one temple but a monumental five-acre complex of temples.

Although Karnak reached its height as Egypt's ceremonial capital during the New Kingdom, it was in fact located on a spot that had been considered sacred long before. So powerful has the site's hold been over the Nile Valley's inhabitants that even to those of the Early Dynastic Period it was a place of power dating back to a more remote antiquity, having been settled as early as 3200 BC and having borne the name Ipet-isut, or the "Chosen of Places."

The first known temple rose on the site during the Middle Kingdom, though it has not survived. The ruins visible today date from the New Kingdom, when Pharaohs Thutmose I and Thutmose III and Queen Hatshepshut laid the groundwork for a temple befitting the growing prestige of Amen. Lesser additions by later rulers only further set the stage for what would become the architectural linchpin in the complex, the Great Hippostyle Hall, completed during the reign of Ramses II in the thirteenth century BC.

The most imposing of the many temples at Karnak, the Hippostyle Hall is also among the largest single chambers ever built and could easily accommodate the entire cathedral of Notre Dame within its walls. A veritable forest of 134 stone columns supported the roof, each column decorated with carvings showing the pharaohs worshiping Amen. The hall's outer walls were similarly carved with scenes trumpeting the victories of Ramses II and his father, Seti I, over Egypt's enemies.

Karnak was the enclave of Egypt's royal priesthood and much of it was off-limits to the general public, which had to make do with lesser deities while the priests catered to the King of the Gods. Each day began with the ritual unsealing of the temple sanctuary that housed the statue of Amen. Then the attending priests, like glorified valets, buzzed around the statue, dressing it, anointing it with perfume, and finally presenting it with food and drink before resealing the sanctuary.

Several times a year, most notably during the time of the annual Nile floods, Amen was allowed a ceremonial outing, escorted as always by his entourage of priests. In a colorful procession watched by crowds of people, the statue was removed from its shrine and carried to the banks of the Nile. There it was placed aboard a sacred barge for the two-mile journey upriver to the temple of Luxor. After a visit of nearly a month, the statue was returned to Karnak via the same route and accompanied by the same fanfare.

Amen's retinue grew appreciably during the reign of Ramses III, when the pharaoh "donated" 86,486 slaves to the service of the god. By then, too, Amen "owned" sixty-five villages, forty-six building yards, 700,000 acres of land,

Erected around 2000 BC on a site already consecrated by a thousand years of veneration, the ancient Egyptian holy city of Karnak (below) lies in well-preserved ruins some 370 miles south of Cairo. The pharaonic descendants of those who had worshiped there from time immemorial dedicated Karnak to the sun god Amen. In the Temple of Amen, located at the far right corner of the pool, stands a bronze statue of the god in pharaohlike form (inset).

and half a million cattle. None of this, however, was enough to slow this mighty god's fall from grace, his slide coinciding with Egypt's own loss of dominance during the second half of the first millennium BC. Nevertheless, a succession of pharaohs and usurping invaders, including Alexander the Great, continued to pay homage to Karnak.

At some point, time and the river caught up with the complex, the Nile floods slowly gnawing away at the sandstone bases of its walls and columns and gradually reducing it to ruins. It remained that way until the early 1700s, when a French Jesuit priest named Claude Sicard had both the good fortune to stumble upon the site and the good sense to grasp the immensity of his discovery. One of the latter-day mysteries associated with Karnak concerns the extensive manuscript that Père Sicard completed about his find. It was not published during his lifetime, and no trace of it was ever found after his death. Documentary evidence of his great discovery exists only in the form of letters he wrote to friends and a map he drew of Karnak's location. Today, hordes of visitors come not only to gaze in awe on Karnak's ancient architectural wonders but to sense the mystical power that still emanates from its old stones.

More resistant to the ravages of time was the holy city that has been called "the Jerusalem of Ethiopia"—Lalibela. Here, eleven churches, all carved from living rock below the level of the earth's surface, allegedly at the express direction of God, have defied both the effects of age and the attempts of invaders to tear them down. Between and beneath them lies a honeycomb of passageways, caves, and tunnels, one of which is said to offer visitors a symbolic tour of hell. Nearby, too, are a grave that is reportedly the tomb of Adam and a stone at once so heavy that no nonbeliever can lift it and so light that any true believer can raise it with ease.

Lalibela, where all these marvels are clustered, is a remote mountain village that was once Ethiopia's capital and was named for the king who built the churches in the early thirteenth century. According to legend, work on them got under way after King Lalibela had a dream in which Christ appeared to him. Over the next two decades, a small army of stonemasons labored on the structures, assisted, say the legends, by angels, who continued the work at night after the masons had retired for the day.

Looking at Lalibela today, it is easy to understand the need for the intervention of angels, for the churches were not so much built as painstakingly hewn out of pink tuff, volcanic rock fused into a solid mass by intense heat. The workers first had to free the raw material from the rest of the mountainside by cutting a deep trench around a single huge block. The block was then hollowed out to create the church's interior—experts are divided on whether the work progressed from bottom to top or vice versa—the masons carefully chiseling the ceilings, arches, columns, altars, and alcoves from the solid rock. No detail was deemed too minor for attention; many of the churches are adorned inside and out with delicate tracery and exquisite ornamentation.

King Lalibela, for whom the city was named, is said to have poured a fortune into the project and to have slept on rocks and subsisted on roots and herbs while construction was under way. When it was finished, the king, according to legend, abdicated his throne and committed himself to a life of Christian contemplation. After his death at age thirty-five, the Ethiopian church declared him a saint.

In addition to his canonization, King Lalibela's exemplary life won him a lasting place in the hearts of his compatriots. But his claim to immortality rests most firmly on the churches he left behind. Indeed, the fact that they were carved directly from the rocky earth proved to be the holy city's salvation when Ahmed ibn Ibrahim al-Gazi, the infamous El Gran, "the Left-handed," came calling in 1527 leading a brutal Islamic jihad, or holy war. Behind him lay a trail of demolished churches and slain priests, as well as thousands of new Ethiopian Muslims, converted at sword point. Lalibela's rock-hewn churches proved impervious to El Gran's strong-arm tactics, and they survive today.

Although militant Islam failed to carry the day in Ethiopia, it was successful in ancient Persia (now Iran), as witness the mystical site originally called Takt-i-Taqdis (Throne of Arches), though its ruins have been known as Takt-i-Suleiman (Throne of Solomon) since Islam supplanted Zoroastrianism as Persia's state religion in about 650. The country's holiest pre-Islamic place, it was built on the shore of a reportedly bottomless blue lake. But even to the Zoroastrians, the site was wreathed in ancient mystery, having been held sacred since at least the sixth century BC.

Fire was central to Zoroastrianism, symbolizing as it did the supreme god Ohrmazd. It was the Royal Fire, that of the warriors and kings, that burned at Takt-i-Suleiman in its own fire temple. Around the temple stood large columned halls, part of the holy city built during the years when it was the ceremonial center of the Sassanian Empire, the last pre-Islamic regime. A processional way led from the city's north gate to the fire temple and on to the lake, and after their coronations at the Sassanian capital at Ctesiphon, newly crowned kings made their way along this avenue to be divinely invested before the Royal Fire.

Although sacked by the Byzantines in 624, the city

St. George's (below), one of eleven churches Ethiopian Christians carved out of rock in the thirteenth century to create the subsurface holy city of Lalibela, stands in an excavation forty feet deep. Its symbolic shape—a cross—is best seen from above (left). According to legend, angels helped to chisel out the churches, but history says that Coptic Christians from Egypt, fleeing persecution by the Muslims, probably aided in the backbreaking task.

was rebuilt and renamed by the triumphant Muslims. It flourished until it began its final decline in the twelfth century, eventually sleeping the long sleep of all dead cities until it was rediscovered in 1819.

The same sleep overtook another Middle Eastern place of power, the Oracle of Claros, after its temple and adjoining buildings were toppled by an earthquake in the early Christian era and the ruins were gradually silted over by mud from a nearby stream.

In its prime, Claros, on the west coast of present-day Turkey, had been one of the ancient world's most popular destinations, and those in need of divine counsel beat a path to the oracle in the years following the region's conquest by Alexander the Great in the fourth century BC. In those days, whole cities would consult the oracle on an annual basis, the date becoming the occasion for a festive civic outing led by a choir singing hymns to Apollo.

By that time, too, the temple had been built and dedicated to Apollo. Inside the temple a colossal seated statue of the god was flanked left and right by the standing figures of Artemis and Leto. Directly beneath the statue of Apollo, at the end of a narrow passageway punctuated by six right-angle turns, lay the adytum, the holy of holies, where the priest of Apollo imbibed the water of inspiration before speaking in verse on behalf of the god.

Along the passageway to this low-ceilinged chamber the oracle's patrons were led. To heighten the drama, the consultations took place at night, and the narrowness of the corridor ensured that visitors had to walk in single file, feeling their way by torchlight. Apparently, the faithful were not allowed to enter the adytum itself, but waited nearby in a vaulted hall while a priest slipped into the darkness to partake of the holy water of Claros, "a draught of which," wrote one Roman commentator, "inspires wonderful oracles, but shortens the life of the drinker."

So effective was this pagan holy water that Apollo's go-between could apparently read the minds of the huddled customers, delivering the answers they sought without even bothering to wait for their questions. Although one Cynic philosopher discovered that other clients had been given the same advice he had received, this apparent breach of faith was not well-enough known to shake the conviction of true believers. Reports of the oracle's successes were more widespread, including Apollo's prophecy of the impending doom of Germanicus, the emperor Tiberius's nephew and adopted son—heir to the throne. A year after this prediction, in AD 19, Germanicus was dead.

The Oracle of Claros survived Germanicus, as it had earlier survived the transfer of power in the Hellenistic world from the Greeks to the Romans. Indeed, under Roman rule the oracle gained in prestige and became even more celebrated and more widely known, its fame spreading as far as Britain. Even the coming of Christianity failed to fully silence the oracle, and its priests continued to oblige all comers, until the earth shook, the temple fell, and the voice of Apollo was stilled at last.

The ruins of Apollo's temple and the other buildings have been the subject of several modern excavations, including a French dig in 1950. Each time, the river has undone the painstaking labors of the archaeologists, and the site has gradually silted in again. But a 1913 expedition discovered a cave near the site, its opening in a cliff face about a half-mile from the sanctuary and so far above ground level that it is reachable only with climbing gear. Upon examination, the cave was found to contain a spring and shards of pottery dating as far back as the third millennium BC.

No great leap of imagination is required to speculate that the oracular powers residing at Claros, no matter how forcefully and elaborately they may have been sited in Greek, then Roman, buildings, actually emanated from this mysterious cave. Indeed, the Roman historian Tacitus stated that the true oracle was not in the temple but in a cave.

While earthquakes and silt have rendered the buildings no more than transient phenomena, a true place of power, such as the cave at Claros may be, transcends exigencies of history and even geology. Generations to come may well restore Claros—and other magical places now in abeyance—to positions of respect and veneration.

A Refuge for True Believers

Since colonial times, groups with exotic creeds have sought shelter in the New World. Some, like the Ephrata commune, the Shakers, and the Woman in the Wilderness society, came to America because they thought it would be the site of the Second Coming. Members of the Woman in the Wilderness, for example, built a tabernacle in the state of Pennsylvania in 1694, then took turns sitting on the roof, waiting for the Apocalypse. Their ardor never flagged as the years passed, but their number dwindled to oblivion.

Other groups, including one formed by Cyrus Reed Teed, a charismatic healer of the Eclectic school—a nineteenth-century cult—built out-of-the-way communities so that they could follow their beliefs in private. Teed, who founded the town of Estero, Florida, in the 1890s, preached that the earth was a hollow shell, that our familiar world was located on its inner surface, and that he was the messiah. When he died in 1908, his followers rejoiced, for he had promised to rise and deliver them to heaven. They commenced an expectant vigil over his corpse, but in time the body showed more signs of putrefaction than resurrection, and health officials ordered him buried.

Similar settlements still exist, including Spiritualist communities like the one shown on the following pages, the Southern Cassadaga Spiritualist Camp Meeting Association. Spiritualists regard death not as an end but as a transition, and they believe that it is possible to communicate with those who have made the change.

Where Anything Is Possible

Camp Cassadaga was established in 1894, nineteen years after its founder, George P. Colby, experienced an extraordinary sequence of events. Colby, a medium, said that an Indian spirit named Seneca appeared during a séance in Lake Mills, Iowa, and pressed Colby to hurry to Eau Claire, Wisconsin, to meet Spiritualist T. D. Giddings. Impressed by the urgency of the message, Colby left the next day.

With Giddings, Colby held another séance, in which Seneca supposedly revealed that the pair had been chosen to found a Spiritualist camp in Florida. It was to be situated "on high pine bluffs overlooking a chain of silvery lakes" near Blue Springs.

Colby and Giddings set off without delay. They are said to have received another message in Florida, this time describing a footpath in a nearby wood. As the men followed a trail, they realized they were treading the very ground Seneca had described. Colby obtained a deed for the land and built a house. In time, the first Spiritualist gathering was held there—a three-day meeting that drew a hundred people. Camp Cassadaga was born.

Materializations, trumpet séances (in which messages from beyond emerge from a floating, evanescent trumpet), and other spectacles were said to occur regularly at the camp during its heyday in the 1930s and 1940s. The goings-on today are less theatrical but no less mysterious. "Lots of things that people might consider impossible," says a local businessman, "are possible here."

Itself a common symbol of the supernatural, a black cat (right) serves as a chance emblem of the mystical business ahead as it dawdles in a dirt road leading into the Spiritualist community.

The Colby Memorial Temple (below) is the focal point of the Cassadaga community. A typical Sunday service begins with a hymn and a sermon by the pastor. Then a medium calls out messages from the spirit world to individual members of the congregation

Signs (above) hawk the services of mediums who have se up shop outside the Spiritualist camp in hopes of profiting from its enduring popularity. Longtime Cassadagans, no doubt resenting the competition, question the newcomers' mediumistic abilities

A medium (below) gazes intently into a crystal ball. Cassadagans say that, unlike "mere" fortunetellers, who do not necessarily rely on spirit messages, true mediums use crystal balls only to invoke the other side.

In Touch with the Other Side

Spiritualists visit Camp Cassadaga today for a variety of reasons. Many take part in classes and workshops on metaphysical and spiritual topics. Some suffer from diseases or disabling conditions and seek to be treated spiritually at the Caesar Forman Healing Center. Others picnic or meditate in the parks that embrace Spirit Pond and Lake Colby, bodies of water that enchanted the camp's founders long ago. But most visitors are drawn by a desire to receive spiritual counseling.

Guests are not required to make an appointment in order to see a medium. They can drop in unannounced on certain Saturdays or on Mediums Night, the first Monday of each month, for fifteen-minute "minireadings." Longer, more traditional consultations can be scheduled over the phone. Community members will not recommend mediums; instead, they urge the visitor to permit his or her higher self to guide the choice.

Mediums typically give readings in their small cottage homes. Most sessions are a half-hour to an hour long. Not all of them go well: Mediums admit they have occasional off days, and they say that mischievous spirits sometimes pass along bogus information. Yet some readings are successful enough to shake even the strongest doubters. "I didn't believe it," says former Orlando businessman R. P. Howe of his session with a Cassadaga medium. "I fought it and laughed at it. And I came out a believer because there's no damn way that the things she told me could be known."

Hoping to photograph a spirit, medium Henry Fogel (right) presses unexposed film to his forehead. One of his clearest portraits is of an Indian. "I do not know his name," says Fogel, "He only appeared once."

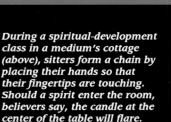

During a spiritual-development class in a medium's cottage (above), sitters form a chain by placing their hands so that their fingertips are touching. Should a spirit enter the room, believers say, the candle at the center of the table will flare.

Gladys Reid (below), a spiritual healer, "lays hands" on a visitor. This contact, says Reid, permits the transfer of her own curative energies, which are merged with those of her "teachers in the other world."

Spiritualist minister Darleen Misskelley (right), former president of Camp Cassadaga, meditates in the tall grass next to Spirit Pond. Misskelley goes there most evenings, she says, "to pray to the moon."

CHAPTER 4

Magic and Mysticism

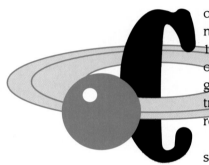

overed with cattle ranches and fields of grain, America's Great Plains feed not only the United States but much of the rest of the world. Until the late 1800s, however, they boasted riches of a far different kind: the buffalo and other wildlife essential to the existence of the Plains Indians. The epic struggle between settlers and Indians for this vast landscape involved diplomacy, trade, battles, and bloody raids—and, in the end, a remarkably widespread resort to Native American magic.

By 1890, the conflict was almost over, the buffalo all but gone. In the summer and fall of that year, an occult movement called the Ghost Dance spread like a prairie fire across the plains. Night after night in Indian villages and camps, flickering fires lit circles of men and women, their fingers interlaced, dancing with shuffling side steps. As they danced, they sang the glories of the well-remembered past, now gone but soon to return if the magic dance succeeded, bringing freedom to roam the boundless grasslands in pursuit of renewed herds of buffalo.

The Ghost Dance they practiced had its origins to the west, in Nevada, where a Paiute named Wovoka had experienced a vision during a solar eclipse in January 1889. In the vision, Wovoka told his followers, a supreme being had shown him the happy life in the land of the dead and had vouchsafed him a view of the future. Summoned by a traditional circular "ghost dance," the dead would soon rejoin the living, Wovoka said; game would return to the land, and all would live in abiding peace with the whites.

The Paiute spread Wovoka's message enthusiastically to other peoples, who changed the interpretation to mean that the return of the buffalo would coincide with the departure or extermination of the whites. The Sioux added their own touches to the dance, circling faster and faster until some participants fell into trances. Some then saw visions that assured them that special powers would help the Ghost Dancers to kill whites. Many also took to wearing ghost shirts or ghost dresses, white garments decorated with spiritual emblems thought to provide magical protection against bullets.

Many Indians slipped away from the reservations onto which the government had herded them to join their comrades at Ghost Dance gatherings.

Despite their now pitifully diminished military power, their antiwhite movement spread alarm among authorities. On December 15, 1890, Daniel Royer, the agent at Pine Ridge in South Dakota (whom the Sioux called Young-Man-Afraid-of-Indians), telegraphed for help. "Indians are dancing in the snow and are wild and crazy," he told his superiors. "We need protection and we need it now." Among the forces that soon arrived to fight off the magic dance were military units armed with Gatling guns.

By that time, winter's onset had forced many of the Sioux back to the hated reservations. On their way to the Pine Ridge Agency, one group of 350 men, women, and children led by Big Foot (also known as Spotted Elk) was intercepted by troops of the Seventh Cavalry, who took them to an army encampment at Wounded Knee Creek. On the morning of December 29, the soldiers there demanded that the Indian men surrender their guns.

Surrounded by 500 soldiers, the Sioux must have suspected that their ghost shirts would soon be put to the test. Tensions rose as soldiers approached the Indians and began to search beneath the blankets they wore as protection against the bitter winter wind. A medicine man known as Yellow Bird exhorted the Sioux warriors to stand fast. "Do not be afraid. I have received assurance that their bullets cannot penetrate us; the prairie is large and the bullets will not go toward you; they will not penetrate you."

Suddenly, a gun went off, triggering pandemonium. Warriors rushed to their families as an artillery barrage swept the Indian camp. A few Indians returned fire, but most took refuge in a nearby ravine. When the artillerymen moved their guns to rake this area, the survi-vors fled on foot; many later succumbed to wounds, cold, or exhaustion miles from Wounded Knee.

By noon, when the firing ended, 25 soldiers were dead, some killed in their own cross fire. How many Indians died will never be known, but the total probably approached 300, including many women and children. With them died the last hopes of the Ghost Dancers for the magical restoration of a lost world.

Feared despite its vulnerability to modern bullets, the Ghost Dance reveals the enduring role of magic in human affairs, with its persistent power to excite both conviction and terror. With rituals that vary from dances to human sacrifice to the use of charms and spells, peoples around the world still seek to harness supernatural forces. The goals of such rites are fairly constant—to heal, to predict the future, to attract a love or destroy an enemy, even, as in the Ghost Dance, to preserve a way of life. But the magic used for those ends is highly localized, and like colored patches on a map of the planet, the occult traditions of each part of the world form a global mosaic, of which no two pieces are quite the same.

At the world's natural cross-roads, still other magical practices have developed through

111

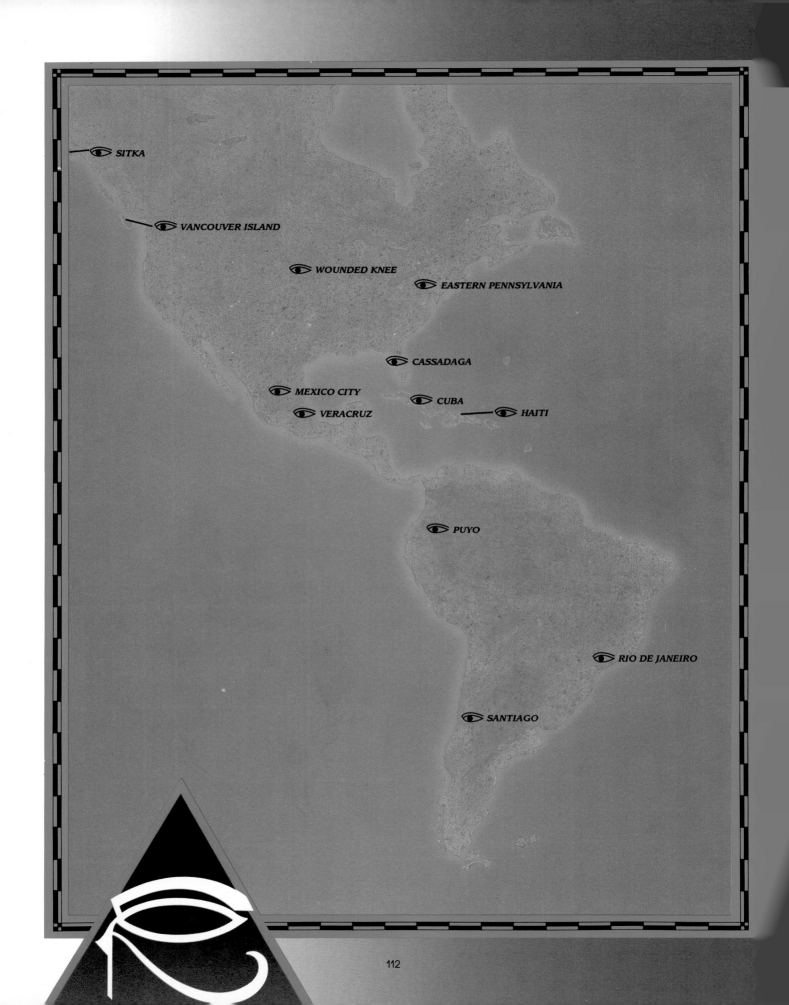

SITKA

VANCOUVER ISLAND

WOUNDED KNEE

EASTERN PENNSYLVANIA

CASSADAGA

MEXICO CITY

CUBA

HAITI

VERACRUZ

PUYO

RIO DE JANEIRO

SANTIAGO

a blending of the beliefs of different lands to form unique hybrid rituals. More than 2,000 years ago, for example, the trading city of Alexandria, Egypt, fused ideas from East and West to create a new kind of alchemy and astrology. And in the nineteenth century, the black slaves of the Caribbean and South America combined African and European ideas to forge a variety of lasting religiomagical traditions, from voodoo in Haiti to macumba in Brazil and santería in Cuba.

Santería, literally the "way of the saints," is thought to have evolved in the 1800s from an amalgam of diverse occult influences that came together in the steamy sugar fields of Cuba. A magical set of religious beliefs that deifies the forces of nature, santería combines elements of the Yoruba culture of those dragged into slavery from West Africa with the traditions of the Catholic church, in which owners were required by law to instruct their slaves.

Like voodoo, a similar syncretic faith with which it is often compared, santería involves personified forces of nature. These, known as *ori-*shas, are also identified with a particular human quality and with a corresponding Catholic saint. Changó, for instance, one of the most powerful and popular of the orishas, controls fire, thunder, and lightning, is identified with Saint Barbara, and symbolizes control over enemies and adversity. Oshún, also revered as the Virgin of Charity, governs river waters and in human endeavors stands for love, fertility, and gold.

Like the ancient Yoruba tradition from which it grew, santería is based on the concept of *ashé,* or divine power. Ashé can solve problems, subdue enemies, and ensure love and wealth. Human access to this force comes by way of the orishas and is acquired through invocations, propitiations, spells, and rituals.

Devotees, who are known as *santeros,* frequently approach the orishas with offerings of fruits, flowers, candles, and food, because the orishas, for all their power, still must eat to survive. Only when human life or other vital issues are at stake do worshipers provide blood sacrifices of a chicken,

The Loa Danh, a Haitian voodoo talisman said to bring great wealth

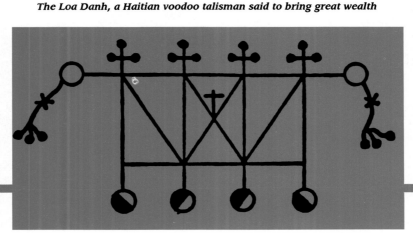

The Occult Americas

CASSADAGA
While conducting a séance in the late 1800s, George P. Colby received a message instructing him to form this northern Florida Spiritualist community, which now draws visitors from all over the United States.

CUBA
In the santería belief system that evolved on this Caribbean island, lives are viewed as predestined. The faithful can realize their fates with the help of spirits invoked through dance, sacrifices, and other rituals.

EASTERN PENNSYLVANIA
German immigrants to this area in the seventeenth and eighteenth centuries brought with them a belief that hex signs painted on barns could protect crops and families from witchcraft.

HAITI
The voodoo faith that developed in this Caribbean nation includes a strong fear of supernatural forces. Protection from capricious spirits is a daily worry for most believers.

MEXICO CITY
This city is built on the site of Tenochtitlán, the Aztec capital, which once witnessed daily human sacrifices. Aztec myth held that the sun died every night and could be reborn only if it was fed with human blood.

PUYO
Near this town in Ecuador live the Jívaro Indians, known for shrinking the heads of their enemies. In other rites, the Jívaro seek knowledge of spirits and other beings by ingesting datura, a natural narcotic.

RIO DE JANEIRO
Devotees who practice macumba, a magic common to this Brazilian state and city, use white magic to cast healing and love spells. Macumba priests also divine the future with seashells and coconuts.

SANTIAGO
On the Andean slopes near this Chilean city lie shrines where Incas once sacrificed children to the sun and to their creator god Viracocha. The death of these willing victims allegedly assured good fortune for all.

SITKA
The Tlingit people who live near this city and throughout the Alaskan Panhandle believe that their shamans' contact with the spirit world produces great catches of fish as well as other windfalls.

VANCOUVER ISLAND
During lunar eclipses, Kwakiutl Indians on this Canadian island burn hair and old clothes in the traditional belief that the reeking blaze will make the sky sneeze and free the moon from the mouth of heaven.

VERACRUZ
Indian paper magic practiced in this southern Mexican state utilizes paper figures that represent spirits. Shamans tear up images of evil spirits to banish them but keep seed-spirit figures to ensure good crops.

WOUNDED KNEE
In 1890, the massacre of about 300 Sioux men, women, and children at this South Dakota creek effectively ended the Ghost Dance movement, once seen as a magical route back to the pre-European way of life.

a sheep, or some other animal, which is later eaten by the congregation.

During some ceremonies, the unseen orishas are invited to join the santeros in singing and dancing. Sometimes an orisha may choose to "seize the head" of one of the performers, an event often signaled by dancing that is said to be far more spectacular than any the human medium could perform in ordinary consciousness. Speaking through the possessed dancer, the orisha often delivers messages and advice to those who are present. Orishas may also be consulted indirectly through a rite called Ifa, in which patterns of thrown bone fragments imply the answer

to a petitioner's problems; the solution is couched in terms of a story involving an orisha or hero from ages past.

Less frequently, a santero may use magical spells to invoke the power of an orisha, particularly the powerful Changó. In one case reported in 1989 by anthropologist and santería initiate Migene González-Wippler in her book *Santería: The Religion,* a New York City nightclub owner received a series of anonymous threats aimed at forcing him out of business. Discovering that the threats came from the owner of a rival nightclub, the man turned to a santero for help. The santero cast a spell by mixing together several magic powders, which were wrapped in red silk and scattered at the enemy's door at midnight. He then lit a red candle in honor of Changó and burned a photo of the rival's nightclub in its flame. A few weeks later, a fire devastated the other club. The New York City fire department blamed faulty wiring, but the santería faithful gave credit to Changó.

As that story suggests, santería is no longer restricted to Cuba itself. After the Cuban Revolution of 1959, santería went on the move, spreading with more than a million Cuban exiles who poured into Venezuela, Puerto Rico, and the United States. By the 1980s, New York City had more than a hundred specialty shops, or *botánicas,* catering to the needs of santería ritual, and there were at least eighty such stores in Miami, Florida. In those cities and other towns, expatriate Cuban worshipers continue to invoke the orishas, sometimes thousands of miles from their island home.

Echoes of a more brutal American magic linger in the remains of Tenochtitlán, capital city of the old Aztec Empire of central Mexico. Built on an island at the center of Lake Texcoco, the same site now occupied by Mexico City, Tenochtitlán spread over nearly five square miles. Well-ordered canals and streets linked neighborhoods that housed more than half a million inhabitants. The city center was dominated by a tall pyramid topped by shrines to the rain god Tlaloc and to Huitzilopochtli, patron god of the Aztecs. At those shrines, the Aztecs regularly performed rituals thought to replenish the powers of the sun, rituals soaked in human blood.

Even as Tenochtitlán reached its peak, it came under assault by the invading army of Spanish conquistador Hernán Cortés in 1519. Within two years, Cortés conquered the Aztecs and destroyed their proud capital. Before the Spanish prevailed, however, a sergeant named Bernal Díaz del Castillo watched the grisly Aztec sacrifice of several of his compatriots. Díaz del Castillo reported that the men, who had been captured in a recent battle, were first dragged up the steps of the temple by warriors and priests, then dressed in Aztec costumes and forced to dance before an idol of the nation's patron god. Finally, the priests placed the Spaniards on their backs on narrow sacrificial stones and with sharp flint knives "sawed open their chests and drew out their palpitating hearts and offered them to the idols that were there."

Historians believe that many tens of thousands of Indians, mostly captive warriors from other tribes, had preceded the unfortunate Spaniards to the sacrificial altar over the years. Many went willingly, since death at the hands of the priests was considered an honor. After the ceremony, their bodies were rolled down the steps to ritual experts who dismembered and flayed them. The skin was saved for ceremonial uses, the skulls displayed and the flesh reserved for ritual consumption by the victim's captor and his relatives. The latter practice led in 1970 to a controversial speculation by Michael Harner of the New School for Social Research that the enormous volume of sacrifice at Tenochtitlán may have redressed a protein deficiency in the Aztec diet, as well as honoring the Aztec gods.

Whatever the origins of Aztec human sacrifice, that particular magical rite ended with their defeat. Lesser known Aztec beliefs about the spirit world may still endure, however, in the so-called paper magic of the Nahua Indians who live in the remote, forested mountains of Mexico's Veracruz province. The Nahua, who are thought to be descended from the Aztecs, see no conflict between their magic and the Roman Catholicism they also practice, but they usually hide their non-Christian observances from less flexible outsiders.

In their magic rituals, the Nahua employ paper images called *tlatecme,* cut by shamans to represent various spirits from the Nahua pantheon. When immersed in the smoke of copal incense, a paper cutout is said to attract its corresponding spirit. A Nahua shaman then manipulates the life force of the spirit to effect cures, increase crops, produce rain, or practice sorcery.

A commonly depicted group of spirits are the *ejecatl,* wind spirits feared by the Aztecs and considered responsible for disease and other misfortune such as drought and barrenness. These spirits are said to lurk near houses, trails, and other places where people are to be found, seeking to

egg, tobacco, and cornmeal. He then picks up a bundle of tlatecme and herbs, thrusts it into a cloud of incense, rubs it over the patient, and tears it to shreds, chanting "Xiahque Ejecatl!" ("Begone, wind!") and other dismissive phrases. Similar rituals may be repeated throughout the day. When all the wind spirits have been lured to their paper images and torn apart, the patient evidently stands a good chance of recovery; Nahua shamans are judged by their results.

To the south of the Nahua and the lands their ancestors may have ruled lie the soaring Andes, mountain spires of the Inca Empire that once held most of western South America. The Incas left their mark on the land they once dominated, nowhere more so than in the Andes. From these exalted peaks, according to tradition, came many of the *huacas,* the Incas' god-ancestors, whose shrines (also called huacas) are still to be found on the steep upper slopes. Sometimes the mountains yield up other evidence of the Incas' religious devotion: the bodies of sacrificial victims, left to die half a millennium ago and mummified by the cold, dry winds. These grisly discoveries bear mute testimony to a culture that gladly offered the lives of beautiful, highborn children to placate the gods.

The clearest evidence of ancient Inca sacrificial practices is the well-preserved body of a young boy, probably from the fifteenth century, which was discovered in 1954 more than 17,000 feet up an Andean peak northeast of Santiago, Chile. Curled on his side under a huge slab when discovered, the child wears llama-wool clothing and heavy silver jewelry that signify noble birth. By his side were found figurines of gold, silver, and shell, and a feathered bag of coca leaves that may have numbed him as he died, most likely from the cold. The boy's face is composed in an expression of great peace.

It is plain that in his short life the boy had been imbued with the beliefs and spiritual customs that controlled virtually every aspect of Inca life. It was reckoned a great honor to die to ensure the king's prosperity and that of the empire he ruled. The sacrificial victim was also thought to be transformed by death into a new deity, to be consulted in

enter the bodies of the unsuspecting. Although other treatments may be provided for those fallen ill from such attacks, a complete cure requires special cleansing rituals, performed in a room filled with the smoke from a clay incense burner. The presiding shaman cuts dozens of tlatecme from folded sheets of paper he brings with him—colored paper for the ejecatl and white paper for other spirits that will witness the cleansing.

After some preliminary rites, the shaman arranges the paper images in a circle atop bunches of sacred plants and sprinkles the paper with offerings such as white rum, raw matters as diverse as agriculture and personal health.

Hundreds of other children, perhaps thousands, died every year in such service to the empire before it crumbled under the Spanish onslaught in 1532. And, although Spanish priests spared no efforts to stamp out every vestige of the old religion, there is evidence that human sacrifice has continued in the modern era. Time and commerce have corrupted the rituals, however. Children no longer happily meet their end for the good of the community, and whole villages rarely gather to make their offering to the gods. Instead, some smugglers, mine owners, and businesspersons in remote areas lure youths into the mountains. The teenagers discover too late that they themselves will be the object of the fatal rite, which is meant to prevent mining cave-ins or other ill fortune.

Where the Andes bend toward the misty forests of the Amazon basin, mountain waterfalls and swift, rocky streams pierce a remote wooded wilderness. This isolated region of Ecuador is the home of the Jívaro, the only Indian tribe in South America that successfully resisted the conquering armies of the Spanish Empire.

After an early period of informal Spanish settlement, the Jívaro rose against the newcomers in a bloody and successful revolt in 1599, then withstood all further attempts to subjugate them despite the known presence of rich gold deposits in the area. The Jívaro kept their independence in part because their mountainous domain, protected by unnavigable rivers to the east and a steep escarpment to the west, made invasion difficult. Still more daunting was their warlike reputation—and their age-old custom of collecting and shrinking the heads of their defeated enemies.

The defense of their freedom was not the only reason for the Jívaro's bellicosity, a quality for which they are still known today. Every Jívaro warrior relies on spiritual powers to protect him from physical violence, poison, and sorcery. Warriors long maintained their powers by joining killing forays against neighboring villages or isolated dwellings. The purpose was to collect human heads. Although the

practice became less common in the twentieth century, it continued through the late 1960s and may not be entirely abandoned today.

Under no circumstances could the killers fail to take their victims' heads, for each might harbor a *muisak,* an avenging soul released by the act of murder. To protect himself from the muisak, a trophy-taking Jívaro warrior had to trap it inside the head. The first step was to remove the skin and hair, discarding the skull; the scalp was then

An Otomí shaman from Mexico's Veracruz province drizzles chicken blood over paper figures. Supposedly, evil wind spirits will be drawn to the blood-soaked images and then dispersed when the paper is ripped to pieces.

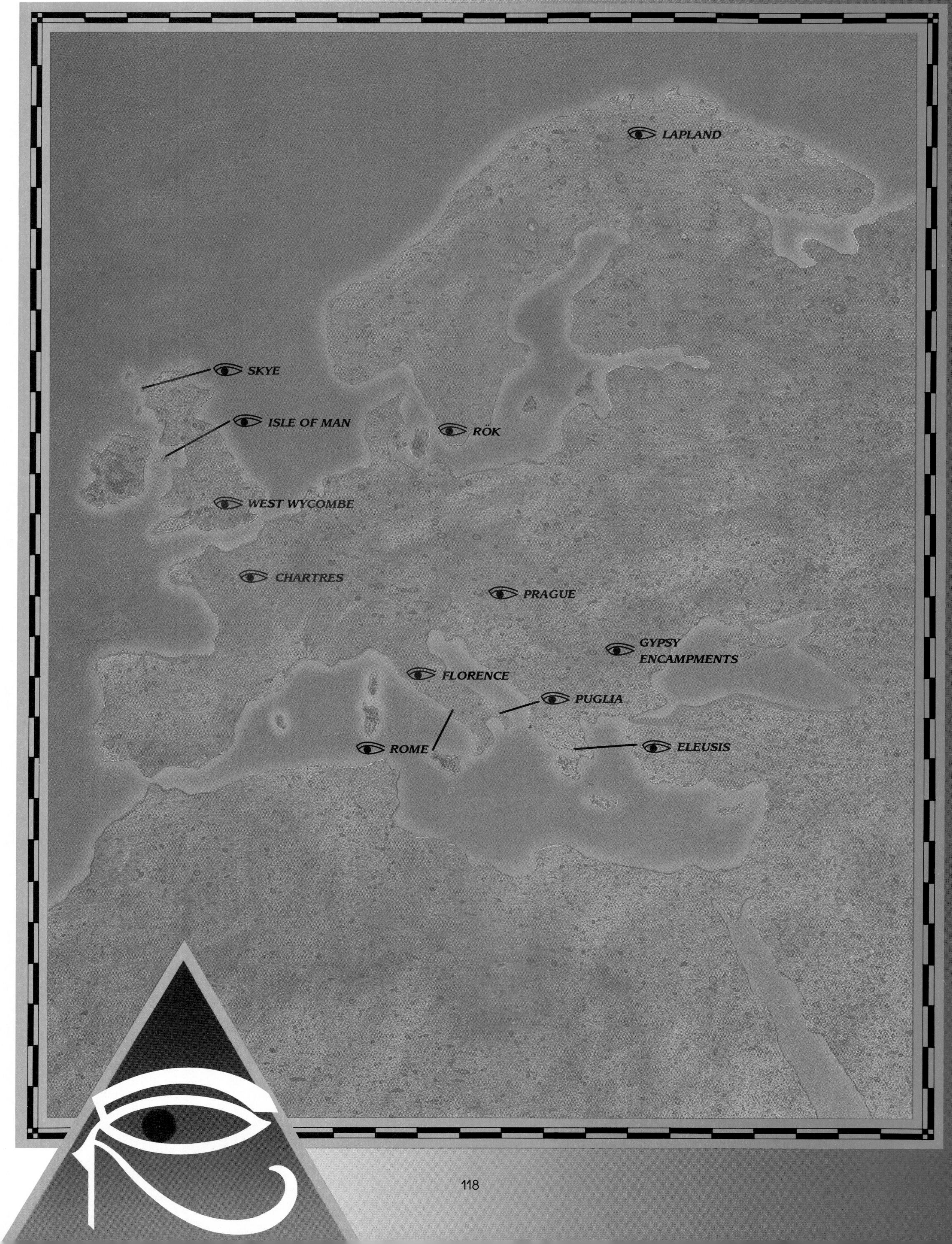

SKYE

ISLE OF MAN

WEST WYCOMBE

CHARTRES

RÖK

LAPLAND

PRAGUE

GYPSY
ENCAMPMENTS

FLORENCE

PUGLIA

ROME

ELEUSIS

boiled in water and shrunk by means of heated stones and sand. Eyelids and mouth were sewn shut to keep the muisak from escaping. The end result was a shriveled object, known as a *tsantsa*, little larger than a man's fist.

At feasts to celebrate the taking of another's head, the potency of the imprisoned muisak was put to use. During a ritual dance, a head taker conferred the muisak's power on two female relatives, usually his wife and his sister, to enable them to work harder and more productively. Only after several feasts over a period of as much as two or three years would the muisak be allowed to depart in a formal ceremony. The shrunken head, no longer of any significance, was once discarded; in the twentieth century, however, it became a sought-after souvenir. Today, shrunken heads are a staple Jívaro export, although most if not all of those sold as human are in fact created from goat or other animal skins by Ecuadoran craftspeople.

Although foreign collectors delight in the macabre thrill of owning a shrunken head, ritual magic is

hardly confined to such out-of-the-way places as the Ecuadoran rain forest. The eminently modern nations of Europe have also fallen heir to ancient secret arts, some no longer practiced and some, like astrology, supremely popular.

In the continent's northernmost reaches, for example, a nomadic people known as the Lapps (sometimes referred to as the Sami) once roamed in bands through a forbidding land of mountains, tundra, forests, and lakes. Fishing, hunting, and tending their large herds of reindeer, they made the most of their arctic domain, where winter was always long, dark, and cold. For centuries, their openly held pagan beliefs represented one of the last bastions of old European magic against the spread of Christianity.

Bears, the largest and most dangerous game animals of the Arctic, were sacred creatures to the Lapps. Not only was the bear's winter-long hibernation a mystery, but its ability to walk on its hind legs gave rise to the idea that the bear was partly human. In response, the Lapps gave the bear special names—Grandfather, Woolly One, Honey Paws—and

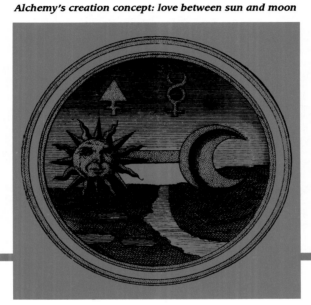

Alchemy's creation concept: love between sun and moon

Europe's Occult Centers

CHARTRES
The great cathedral here not only reflects the occultism practiced in ancient times but also harbors another mystery: How did its builders gain the know-how to erect such a perfectly proportioned building?

ELEUSIS
Ceremonies called Mysteries, performed in this Greek town from about 1900 BC onward, began as fertility rites but later took on an occult flavor, with darker, more complex interpretations about the afterlife.

FLORENCE
A bright jewel of the Renaissance, this city under Cosimo I and Francesco I de' Medici fostered important advances in science and medicine that grew out of the Medici passion for alchemy, astrology, and magic.

GYPSY ENCAMPMENTS
From their camps on the edges of towns, nomadic gypsies spread the art of palmistry across medieval Europe. The Church outlawed the practice in the 1600s but succeeded only in driving it underground.

ISLE OF MAN
Once ruled, it is said, by a giant with magical powers, later the site of witch burnings, this island in the Irish Sea was chosen by Gerald Gardner, father of modern witchcraft, as an apt place to spend his last years.

LAPLAND
This region of Arctic Europe has long been known for sorcery. So eerie did the Lapps' shamanistic ways appear to Christians that these nomads earned an undeserved reputation for potent witchcraft.

PRAGUE
Holy Roman Emperor Rudolf II made this the European hub of alchemy by inviting or dragooning more than 200 practitioners here. They clustered around a single street, which came to be called Golden Lane.

PUGLIA
Trulli—houses with cone-shaped roofs in this region of southeastern Italy—are adorned with symbols to fend off the evil eye, which some can supposedly cast on victims by staring at them or by praising them.

RÖK
The inscription at this Swedish site consists of 720 runes— ancient Scandinavian symbols conveying mystical ideas—the longest ever found. Of all the known runes, more than three-fifths are Swedish.

ROME
For three centuries, writing on the Magic Door in the Piazza Vittorio purportedly has told how to make gold. But neither the marquis of Palombara, who put up the door, nor anyone else has deciphered the script.

SKYE
Some MacLeods credit the magical power of their clan's Fairy Flag not only for their long tenure on this Scottish isle but also for the family's growth— there are 20,000 MacLeods in the United States alone.

WEST WYCOMBE
Near this Buckinghamshire town was the home of Sir Francis Dashwood, who founded his Hell-Fire Club allegedly for the black arts. The entrance of the club bore a French motto meaning "Do what thou wilt."

developed a complex structure of rituals for the bear hunt.

Lapps hunted for bears in late winter, hoping to kill them as they emerged from their dens. Before the hunt for this revered animal could begin, however, the hunting party had to consult the community's shaman, whose powers allowed him to foretell their success or failure. The shaman performed his divination with a magic drum, a wood-framed instrument covered with the skin of a young reindeer. The skin was decorated with figures drawn in red alder-bark juice, representing various divinities as well as people and animals in hunting and fishing scenes.

The shaman first placed a piece of wood or horn called the *arpa* on the tight drumhead, then beat the drum with a small T-shaped piece of reindeer antler. As the drumming continued, the arpa danced about over the painted symbols, then stopped moving and stayed at one spot. Based on the symbol where it came to rest, the shaman would cast his augury.

For some divinations, the shaman kept drumming until the rhythmic beat carried him into a trance, in which he might foretell the outcome of the bear hunt, the prospects for the coming hunting and fishing seasons, the fecundity of the reindeer herd, or the chances of illness within the community. In all these matters, the shaman's forecasts would guide the group's behavior in the coming months. In the sixteenth and seventeenth centuries, stories of Lappish magic led to accusations of witchcraft by the pious governments of the nations that claimed the Lapps' lands, particularly Sweden and Norway. After Christian missionaries began to convert Lapps in large numbers in the late 1600s, the magic drums fell into disuse. Most, although not all, were later destroyed by authorities intent on stamping out pagan cults. Only about eighty examples remain today, silently preserved in museums in Sweden, Norway, and Finland. Modern Lappish dancers and would-be shamans have made new drums, but—publicly at least—the emphasis today is on folk art rather than on actual divination.

Another European magical artifact on display—this one reputedly still as potent as ever—is to be found hundreds of miles to the south at Scotland's Dunvegan Castle. A massive pile built high atop a promontory on the isle of Skye, the castle overlooks a narrow arm of the sea known as Loch Dunvegan. Dunvegan Castle is the ancestral seat of the Clan MacLeod, who have occupied it for more than seven centuries—an extraordinary tenure aided, many say, by a powerful talisman still kept at the MacLeod stronghold.

Unimpressive in appearance, the charm is a tattered piece of brown silk, repaired in places with red stitching and

known as the Fairy Flag. According to MacLeod legend, it was bequeathed to a fourteenth-century chief by his fairy wife when she returned to the fairy realm. Its magic, she told her husband, would save the clan three times: Flown in battle, the flag would summon a host of armed men.

Other accounts also attribute magical powers to the flag but trace it to Harald Hardrada, king of Norway, who is said to have brought the flag back as a holy relic from his days in the service of the Byzantine emperor in Constantinople. According to this story, the flag passed into the hands of a MacLeod ancestor allied with Hardrada after that Norse king died invading Anglo-Saxon England in 1066, shortly before the more successful Norman invasion.

Whatever its origin, the Fairy Flag frequently accompanied the clan into battle, carried with great honor by hereditary keepers who took care to make sure it stayed tightly wrapped. In accordance with the fairy's charm, it was unfurled only in case of utmost peril, a circumstance that allegedly arose twice during the clan wars that raged through the Scottish Highlands in the fifteenth and sixteenth centuries. Tradition has it that the Fairy Flag saved Clan MacLeod in 1490 during the battle of Glendale and in 1578 at the battle of the Spoilt Dyke (named for the dyke under which the slain enemy warriors were buried). The

MacLeods were actually outnumbered during the latter engagement, but it is said that when the Fairy Flag was flown, the enemy were so stunned to suddenly see a great army opposing them that they were soon defeated. That left only one remaining opportunity for magical salvation.

Happily, the clan wars subsided before the Fairy Flag's powers were exhausted, and the flag has never again been displayed in battle. Its powers, however, seem undiminished: During a 1938 fire that gutted a wing of Dunvegan Castle, the flames are said to have bowed before the Fairy Flag as islanders carried it to safety.

While Dunvegan's flag offers white, protective magic to the MacLeods, rumors of a far darker art once hung over Medmenham Abbey, an English house leased in 1751 by Sir Francis Dashwood, owner of the nearby Buckinghamshire estate of West Wycombe Park. Medmenham, a large, ivy-covered house, stands serenely on the banks of the Thames, about thirty miles west of London. In Dashwood's day, the tranquil old abbey became the meeting place of a peculiar social club whose practices, some believed, included the celebration of Black Masses. Popular rumor called it the Hell-Fire Club.

To its members, however, the brotherhood was

The Grand Dukes of Alchemy

In the bubbling intellectual stewpot that was sixteenth-century Florence, one fascinating corner of ferment was the alchemical laboratory of the grand duke himself, Cosimo I de' Medici. There, the duke was said to work "with all manner of fires, ovens and alembics," making "remedies to improve health" and seeking to "discover astonishing secrets of nature, which includes the investigation of metals."

Cosimo's devotion to the alchemical quest—and his generous patronage of other alchemists—made Renaissance Florence a center for the "sublime science." So ardent was his pursuit that his adviser on art feared smoke from the laboratory might harm the Palazzo Vecchio's paintings. Indeed, in 1556 the duke's ovens did cause a large fire, but it was extinguished in time to avert a cultural disaster.

His son Francesco I inherited Cosimo's passion for alchemy. Grand Duke Francesco claimed he had solved the problem of perpetual motion, had concocted a cure for the plague, and could turn salt into saltpeter, used in gunpowder. Some of his ingredients were exceedingly peculiar; once he acquired 10,000 scorpions.

As grand duke, he enjoyed advantages unavailable to most alchemists. For example, he tested a potion against poison on condemned prisoners, and none but the prisoners seemed to mind. He did encounter criticism when his pregnant wife, ill after a fall, was given a medicine of his making that contained gold—she died soon thereafter. Still, neither Francesco nor his city gave up their feverish interest in alchemy's mix of science and mysticism.

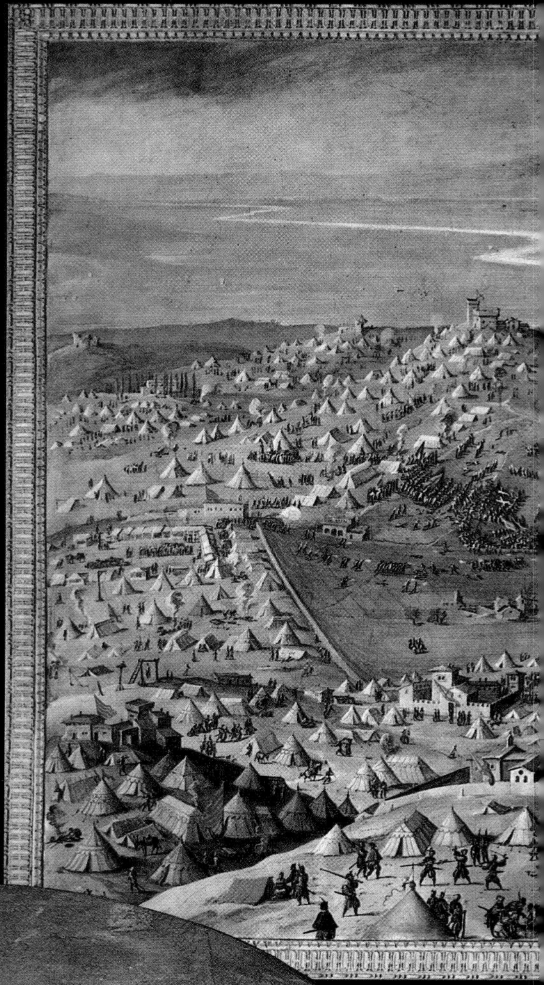

In Florence, the Medici family's Palazzo Vecchio, or "Old Palace"—seen at the left in this eighteenth-century painting— was a focus of alchemy as well as of government and art. The Medicis also dabbled in magic.

ANCISCVS MED·FLOR·ET·SENAR·PRINC

Banners fluttering, troops
besiege Florence in a successful
1529 campaign to return the
Medicis to power after rivals
had ousted them. Alchemists
helped to create weapons for
the era's frequent wars.
Francesco I himself invented an
explosive grenade called Scac-
ciadiavoli, "Devil Crusher," but
apparently it was not used for
fear it might damage the
thrower more than the target.

Francesco I (above) was so en-
grossed in alchemy, as well as
in the arts and sciences in general, that he neglected his political duties, allowing corruption
and disarray to flourish in his
administration and thus speed-
ing his family's eventual down-
fall. In the 1570 painting at
left, he is said to be seen at
the lower right stirring molten
metal over a blazing stove in
an alchemical laboratory.

Framed and mounted, the tattered Fairy Flag (above) still hangs in Scotland's Dunvegan Castle (left), home of Clan MacLeod. Despite the flag's derelict appearance, faith in its protective magic runs strong: Clan members going off to World War II reportedly took tiny pieces of the banner along with them for good luck.

known as the Franciscans of Medmenham, a title coined from Dashwood's first name. A Tory member of Parliament, Dashwood had a well-deserved reputation as a rake and general hell-raiser. As a young man, for instance, he took part in a Good Friday service at the Sistine Chapel in Rome—then laid about savagely with a horsewhip during the traditional moment of darkness.

But Dashwood also had a sociable side, and he had no trouble finding friends to establish a succession of clubs, including the so-called Franciscan order at Medmenham, which seemed in many respects a mockery of the genuine article. Instead of the silence of a real Franciscan abbey, the brothers of Medmenham engaged in lively conversation, often over a table groaning with victuals that would never appear in a monastic refectory. Far from spending their time in contemplation, members and visitors might engage in a variety of games, leaf through racy novels in the abbey library, or frolic with a bevy of female guests selected for their beauty and conviviality.

One chamber at Medmenham remained closed to all but an inner circle among the members, and it was there that rumor placed the rites of Satanic worship. These tales, never corroborated, began with a series of attacks on the Medmenhamites by John Wilkes, a former member of the

"Franciscan brotherhood" who broke with his fellows over a political issue. In 1763, Wilkes wrote of the "mysteries of the chapter-room, where the monks assembled on all solemn occasions, the more secret rites were performed and libations poured forth in much pomp to the Bona Dea," a goddess of ancient Rome. Soon, his mild insider's account was elaborated by others, less well-informed, including the author of a sensational 1765 novel. Such tales provided detailed, if probably imaginary, descriptions of Satanic ceremonies to an avid public.

Such publicity had little effect on the noble Franciscans, who continued to meet at Medmenham for their own mysterious purposes. Not until 1778 did Dashwood, then seventy years old, relinquish the lease on the building, which has since been divided into two private homes.

At about the time that he leased Medmenham Abbey, Dashwood's interest in the exotic led him to begin modifying his surroundings at home in Wycombe. He began by adding a huge gold-colored ball, seven yards wide, to the steeple of a church situated on a hill across from his West Wycombe Park estate. The ball came equipped with a circular bench with room for twelve people, and it was rumored that Dashwood and his companions enjoyed boisterous drinking bouts in this churchly hideaway. Others have suggested the golden sphere represents the sun, which may or may not symbolize the risen Christ. The suggestion of sun worship was reinforced in the early 1760s, when Dashwood renovated the church interior to emulate the Temple of the Sun at Palmyra in Syria.

At the base of the hill on which the church stands, Dashwood dug a series of artificial caves, primarily to supply chalk for a road-building project. The caves extended beyond the requirements of quarrying, however. Tradition suggests they housed a Temple of Bacchus, a match for the Temple of the Sun on the hilltop, complete with esoteric carvings in the chalk walls. Dashwood, who added a Gothic facade to the mouth of the caves, enjoyed conducting visitors through the caverns, pointing out an underground stream he named the River Styx.

It seems a far cry from Wycombe and its murky pagan-Satanic reputation to the famous Gothic cathedral of Notre Dame at Chartres in northern France. Dedicated to the Virgin Mary in the thirteenth century, the Chartres cathedral has been heralded as an architectural triumph of the Christian faith, from the lofty proportions of its vaulted arches to the multicolored light pouring through the stained glass of three huge rose windows. Yet close examination of the structure shows that its builders may have had more in mind than the glories of Christianity. They incorporated in the building a mixture of popular beliefs and ancient teachings—including, some say, the occult science of alchemy.

The placement of the structure is notable, for the cathedral at Chartres stands on an ancient sacred site, where prehistoric Frenchmen once built a dolmen of rough stones. Later, Druids chose the site as a center for teaching and worship, a tradition continued by Christians when they first arrived in the third century. Five churches rose on the site, each in its turn destroyed by fire, before construction of the present building, a thirty-year project that employed the skills of an army of masons, glaziers, and sculptors.

Some of their work seems more reminiscent of the dolmen builders than of any Christian teachings. For example, a large rectangular flagstone in one of the transepts was deliberately set at an angle to the other flooring stones. At noon on the summer solstice, a small knob on the stone glows with light, beamed precisely through a clear pane in one of the stained-glass windows. Similarly, there is no orthodox Christian explanation for the labyrinth set in the flagstones of the nave. Medieval worshipers once danced through this forty-foot-wide maze to celebrate church festivals. Some scholars argue the labyrinth, like similar patterns in other cathedrals, may be an

The gilded, hollow globe on the steeple below, big enough for small but drunken gatherings, was added to the West Wycombe church by Sir Francis Dashwood, founder of the so-called Hell-Fire Club. At right, a Hogarth etching based on a portrait devised for another club shows Dashwood as a Franciscan monk, in a play on his first name. Instead of a rosary, the well-known roisterer holds a glass; instead of a crucifix, he contemplates a seductively posed naked woman. In a final joke, Dashwood's drinking companion the earl of Sandwich peers down on the pseudo monk from a halo.

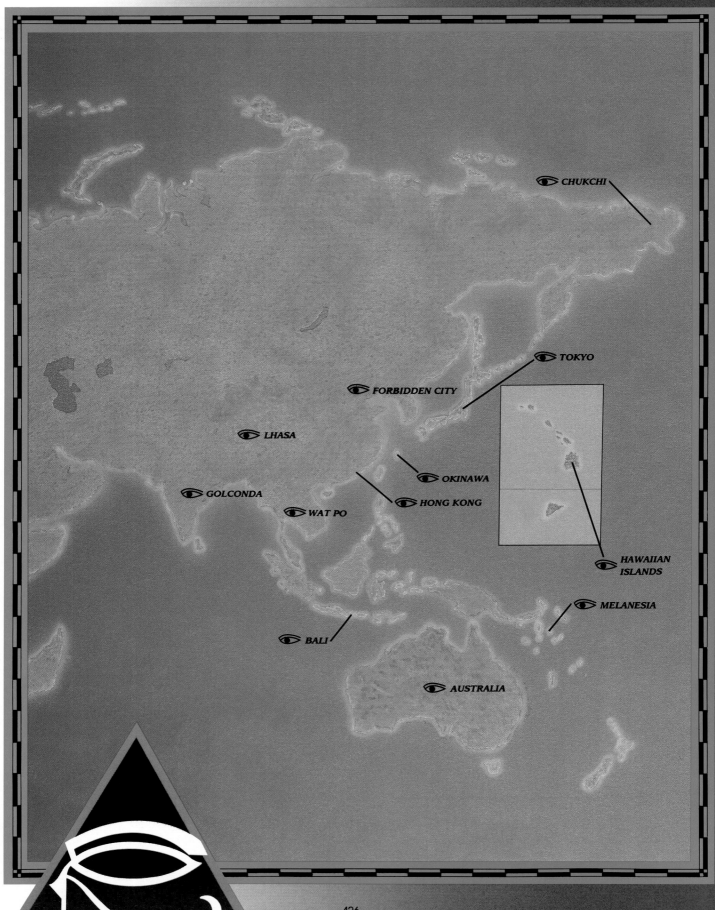

CHUKCHI

TOKYO

FORBIDDEN CITY

LHASA

OKINAWA

GOLCONDA

WAT PO

HONG KONG

HAWAIIAN
ISLANDS

MELANESIA

BALI

AUSTRALIA

emblem of the gold-making "great work" of alchemists who took part in building Chartres.

The foremost proponent of this view was an enigmatic author by the name of Fulcanelli, a modern French alchemist who was rumored to be close to achieving the secret of eternal life. Fulcanelli maintained in his 1926 book *Le Mystère des Cathédrales* that alchemical lore pervaded old Gothic cathedrals.

Fulcanelli believed the lighting of a cathedral like Chartres evoked the color progressions of the Great Work. One rose window, always in shade, symbolized *nigredo,* the blackening or putrefaction of a substance. Another caught the noonday sun, signifying *albedo,* whitening or rebirth; the glow of a sunset through the third rose window was *rubedo,* the reddening or final perfection.

Whatever the truth of Fulcanelli's claims, his theory had some grounding in reality, for European alchemists have never been hesitant about recording the details of their secret art, always in heavily encoded form. A well-known example is the so-called Magic Door of Rome, which is still displayed in the Piazza Vittorio, the site of one of Rome's largest open-air markets.

The Magic Door was commissioned by the marquis of Palombara in 1680, after the nobleman discovered an ancient manuscript that contained a formula for making gold written in cabalistic and astrological symbols. Unfortunately, he was unable to decipher the code. In the hope that some future scholar might succeed where he had failed, the marquis had the formula itself engraved on three pieces of marble placed in a wall at what was then the entrance to his garden. The wall is now part of the piazza's public space. Although the doorway offers its secrets to thousands of visitors every day, no one has yet succeeded in seizing the key to the Great Work.

Long a synonym for occult mystery to Europeans, the distant lands of Asia and the Pacific are indeed home to a multitude of paranormal arts. One ancient tradition that is still widely practiced is the discipline of *feng shui* (Chinese for "wind" and "water"), a magical system of architecture and building placement that

Chinese ideogram for qi, or "cosmic breath"

The Occult Life of the East

AUSTRALIA
The Aborigines here practice many magic rites, including cursing their enemies by muttering over skewers in the ground. Supposedly, the cursed person will suffer whatever bad luck the mutterer described.

BALI
Demons and gods dominate the culture of this Indonesian island, where special ceremonies meant to please the gods or ward off the demons mark every aspect of life from childbirth to cremation after death.

CHUKCHI
Personal guardian spirits supposedly protect the people of the Chukchi region in northern Siberia. They invoke the spirits with human-shaped tattoos and magic necklaces of charms.

FORBIDDEN CITY
This complex in Beijing reflects a tenet of Chinese astrology: Just as the heavens revolve around the North Star, so China was said to turn upon the Dragon Throne at the Forbidden City's center.

GOLCONDA
At least two ill-fated gems originated in this region of southern India: the Koh-i-noor, which changed hands only through theft, murder, or conquest, and the Hope diamond, said to bring disaster to its owners.

HAWAIIAN ISLANDS
Traditional Polynesian sorcerers known as kahunas once imposed supposedly fatal curses, interpreted dreams, and healed the sick. The kahunas' magical healing rites are still occasionally reported.

HONG KONG
In 1963, newspapers in this British colony reported an apparently successful use of the I Ching, an ancient Taoist divination technique; anxious parents had used the oracle, they said, to locate a lost child.

LHASA
The chief city of Tibetan Buddhism until the Dalai Lama fled to India in 1959, Lhasa was once home to mystics supposedly capable of walking on water, floating on air, and bringing back the dead.

MELANESIA
The cargo cults in this chain of islands once built docks for the great ships they expected to bring gifts from the gods; today they more often construct landing strips, assuming the "cargo" will come by air.

OKINAWA
When a fifteenth-century king outlawed the carrying of weapons on this Japanese island, his subjects invented karate, or "empty-hand" combat, a martial art that took on spiritual as well as physical dimensions.

TOKYO
Japan's "new religions," or shinkō shūkyō, are strongest in big cities like this one, where the stress of urban life is answered in part by the magical cures and mediumistic practices of these novel rites.

WAT PO
Thailand's designated center for folk medicine, this Bangkok temple is the source of several traditional texts, including one that prescribes herbal remedies based in part on the day of the week and the taste of the herb.

China's ancient Forbidden City *(far left)* and the ultra-modern Hong Kong and Shang-hai Bank Building *(near left)* in Hong Kong share a common influence, the occult discipline of feng shui. Consultants in the arcane art helped determine the structure, site, and even the opening date for the forty-seven-story skyscraper, completed in the mid-1980s.

is said to use location of objects and structural features to bring good fortune.

The fundamental tool for feng shui (pronounced "fung shway") surveying is a specialized compass inscribed with cosmic symbols. Moving around a potential building site with compass in hand, a feng shui master reads the shapes and positions of surface features to find subterranean "yellow springs," pools of the cosmic breath called *qi* or *ch'i,* that are said to stream over the earth on currents of water and wind. Unlike malevolent "wind spirits" feared by Mexico's Nahua shamans, cosmic breath is beneficial to towns, houses, and tombs—if the structures are placed in the proper orientation to take advantage of the flow of qi. To ensure wealth, for example, a house should be placed inside the curve of a river; general good fortune is thought to come to a house situated among four mountains.

Perhaps the most extraordinary expression of feng shui principles is the 250-acre Forbidden City in Beijing, constructed in the early 1400s by a million laborers who took sixteen years to complete the job. Situated at the center of the Chinese capital, the walled imperial precinct is a model of careful planning, its buildings capped with yellow tile roofs alternating in precise patterns with gleaming white marble terraces and lush gardens. The central building is the formidable Hall of Supreme Harmony, arrayed according to the rules of feng shui to create a place of natural balance "where earth and sky meet, where the four seasons merge." Aligned on a north-south axis, the hall also incorporates elements in each of the five colors thought to pre-

serve harmony: white terraces, black paving stones, red columns, yellow roof, and the natural blue sky overhead.

At the center of the building, surrounded by elaborate staircases, ornate carvings, and gilt pillars, stands the Dragon Throne of the Chinese emperors. By placing it at the focal point of the hall, the architects of the Forbidden City hoped to help their ruler to absorb the cosmic breath that flowed from heaven to the imperial center through Mount Kunlun, a cloud-scraping mountain to the southwest.

Many Asian builders, including those responsible for high-rise construction in modern Hong Kong, South Korea, and even some places in the United States and Europe still turn to feng shui experts for help in finding propitious building sites. The same techniques also serve to diagnose illness and suffering brought on by the negative influences of badly placed residences.

Healing is also the purpose of a number of traditional Asian practices, in which the emphasis is often on curing human ailments through spiritual as well as physical means. A key center for such work is to be found at Wat Po, the oldest of more than 300 temples whose colorful towers pierce the skies of tropical Bangkok, the capital city of Thailand. Constructed in the late 1700s after Bangkok became the capital of what was then Siam, Wat Po serves as a school and library of traditional Thai medicine, which relies heavily on magic for its cures.

Wat Po became a seat of learning during the 1830s, when King Rama III became concerned that the old methods of study, which required long years of individual apprenticeship to a teacher, limited the spread of useful knowledge. Since a lack of printing facilities hampered the distribution of books, important extracts from classic texts were inscribed throughout the temple. The medical library took the form of eighty painted metal statues of revered sages, each demonstrating a physical position designed to relieve a specific ailment—including those caused by spirit possession. Poems and charts on the wall behind each statue offered further explanation of the techniques involved.

To Western eyes, one of the more intriguing statues is the figure depicting John the Baptist, described as a wandering ascetic from the river Jordan, who is shown stretching and healing his own stiff legs. The statue's stooped pose was apparently inspired by the evangelist's biblical statement, passed on by early missionaries to Thailand, that "there cometh one mightier than I after me, the latchet of whose shoes I am not worthy to stoop and unloose."

Traditional Thai healers who gathered at Wat Po were hardly restricted to study of the statues, however; they relied on a variety of esoteric knowledge in such areas as astrology, clairvoyance, exorcism, massage, and pharmacology. Magic incantations were essential to even the most routine herbal cures. For many years these spells were part of the curriculum at Wat Po, but since the late 1950s such teaching has been officially discarded as old-fashioned. This prejudice is not shared by young practitioners, many of whom learn the incantations on their own by seeking out older healers.

At first thought, the highly industrialized island nation of Japan might be expected to be even less hospitable to magic cures than the slowly modernizing establishment at Wat Po. Yet in urban as well as rural settings, Japan's long spiritual traditions persist in rituals reflecting family values and closeness to nature. And in a society made wealthy by the manufacture of modern technology, many people regularly consult with folk healers and fortunetellers.

Although based on ancient ideas, this new healing emerged in its present form after World War II. During the same period that Japan transformed itself into a global eco-

India's Accursed Diamonds

Valued for their beauty and rarity, precious gems throughout the ages have been searched for, bought and sold, stolen, fought over, and, legend has it, cursed—especially two famous stones from India.

Perhaps no gem has a longer history of purported dark powers than the diamond called Koh-i-noor ("Mountain of Light"). Found more than 5,000 years ago in southern India, the stone—weighing almost 800 carats originally—had already been the cause of considerable theft, mayhem, and murder when it was given its lyrical name in 1739 by a Persian despoiler of India, Nadir Shah. He and a succession of despots and brigands—all males—also met ruin or death over the diamond. The British gained possession of it in 1849, and it later became part of the crown jewels. Since then, only female royalty have worn the gem, and no further evil has come of it.

An aura of peril also clings to another Indian gem, the Hope diamond (below). Legend says the fabulous blue stone was stolen from an eye socket of a statue of the Hindu goddess Sita, who laid a curse on it.

Louis XIV of France, who bought the stone in 1668, reportedly died of smallpox after wearing it only once. Louis XVI and his queen, Marie-Antoinette, also wore it; both were beheaded in 1793. Cut to its present weight of 44.5 carats, it was later bought by an Englishman, Henry T. Hope, whose name stuck to it. The last of the Hopes to wear it went bankrupt, and disaster dogged a string of subsequent owners.

In 1911, American heiress Evalyn Walsh McLean purchased the diamond. Two of her children died violently, her marriage collapsed, and her ex-husband went broke and died in a mental hospital. Jeweler Harry Winston bought the stone and in 1958 gave it to the Smithsonian Institution in Washington, D.C., where its alleged powers seem to be in abeyance.

129

nomic superpower, a wide variety of *shinkō shūkyō,* or new religions, took root in the rapidly growing cities. Although most bear some resemblance to such established faiths as Buddhism or Shinto, shinkō shūkyō often reflect ancient Japanese folk beliefs about evil spirits and miracles. Leaders frequently claim magical powers, which they use to help their followers gain divine favor.

Dozens of shinkō shūkyō maintain spiritual centers, or *dojos,* throughout Japan. A typical shinkō shūkyō is Sukyo Mahikari, the True-Light Supra-Religious Organization, with 150 dojos and perhaps 100,000 members in Japan, mostly in the cities. Mahikari attributes most sickness and ill fortune to the action of evil spirits. In keeping with Japanese tradition, the spirits are usually thought to be those of ancestors disgruntled by lack of respect from their descendants, or of animals (most often foxes) seeking to escape the astral world. To contact, placate, and exorcise these influences, worshipers perform a special ritual called *okiyome,* a sort of duet between an investigator and the victim, who acts as a medium for the possessing spirit. Neither is a specialist; Mahikari faithful may take either role.

After a special prayer puts the patient into a trance, the investigator interrogates and scolds the intrusive evil spirit. The possessing spirit usually responds through the patient's voice, although some experienced investigators conduct okiyome silently, reading the mind of the victim to confront the evil spirit. After determining the spiritual cause of the problem being addressed, the investigator then directs purifying energy to appropriate parts of the patient's body. The ritual ends by bringing the subject out of the trance as the spirit is sent back to its own world.

Okiyome has been used to treat ailments from cancer to color blindness, with many claims of miraculous cures. But Mahikari promises its adherents more than health; members have also turned okiyome techniques to such mundane tasks as repairing air conditioners or improving the taste of wine, rice, or noodles. Even the most powerful forces of nature, beyond the reach of modern technology, are said to be susceptible to the cult's magic: a Mahikari dojo supposedly provides certain protection against the destructive typhoons that regularly rake Japan.

Life follows a more leisurely pace far to the south of Japan's hurried cities on the tropical island of New Guinea and its many smaller neighbors. An assortment of islands scattered like green jewels across the Pacific just north and east of Australia, and known collectively as Melanesia, these Pacific lands have always provided for the basic needs of their inhabitants with rich earth, plentiful rainfall, and lush vegetation. For more than a century, however, some Melanesians have expected something more: ships or planes, sent by the gods, filled to overflowing with food, clothing, axes, firearms, boat motors, and other cargo required for the good life, European style.

Hundreds of so-called cargo cults based on this expectation have flourished since the arrival of Westerners in the nineteenth century. A typical movement begins with a prophet who announces a vision promising the imminent return of the spirits of dead ancestors aboard a steamer or airplane crammed with all the goods that whites have been seen to possess in such profusion. The arrival of the ancestors and the cargo will signal the dawn of a new era free of hardship and death. In response to that message, islanders may build a new jetty to accommodate the expected ship or throw together warehouses for the cargo. Routine gardening stops, fruit is harvested, and pigs are slaughtered, all in anticipation of the coming labor-free paradise.

Cargo cults, which continually reappear despite a discouraging lack of results, seem to have arisen from traditional Melanesian attitudes toward wealth. Because social ties between villages or kin groups depended on periodic exchanges of goods and services, failure to meet these obligations brought ineradicable shame. When the Melanesians saw the vast material resources of the Europeans, they anticipated the same relationship with the whites, with industrial-age cargo the most important part of the exchange.

With no concept of the factories that produced the European goods, the Melanesians assumed that cargo, like their own riches of taro and pigs, appeared on earth ready-made as a gift from the gods. When it did not arrive, the islanders usually blamed the failure on fraud by the Europeans, who were thought to have rerouted the ships or mislabeled the crates. It was assumed, however, that the gods would not have allowed such deceit unless the islanders had somehow failed to obey all the strictures issued by the originating prophet. Thus a given cargo cult might subside for years, only to spring up again with the emergence of a new prophet offering hope that with still stricter adherence the dream might finally be realized.

The decades of eager anticipation reached a fulfillment of sorts during World War II, when troops and weaponry arrived on a number of Melanesian islands. New cults quickly formed, and believers built "radio masts," "telegraph lines," and even "telephones" out of vines and other local materials as a way of communicating with the spirit realm; after the war, others drilled with bamboo "rifles" to entice the American soldiers—and their cargo—to return.

With the postwar spread of education and modern in-

Members of a cargo cult on the Melanesian island of Tanna lay flowers at a red cross (right) and pray for the return of John Frum, variously described as a benevolent spirit, the king of America, or a god in human form. Upon his return, say the faithful, a wealth of material goods will arrive, sickness will vanish, gardening will be super-fluous, and Tanna's volcanic mountains, site of an expectant vigil by the lone cultist below, will become fertile riverbeds.

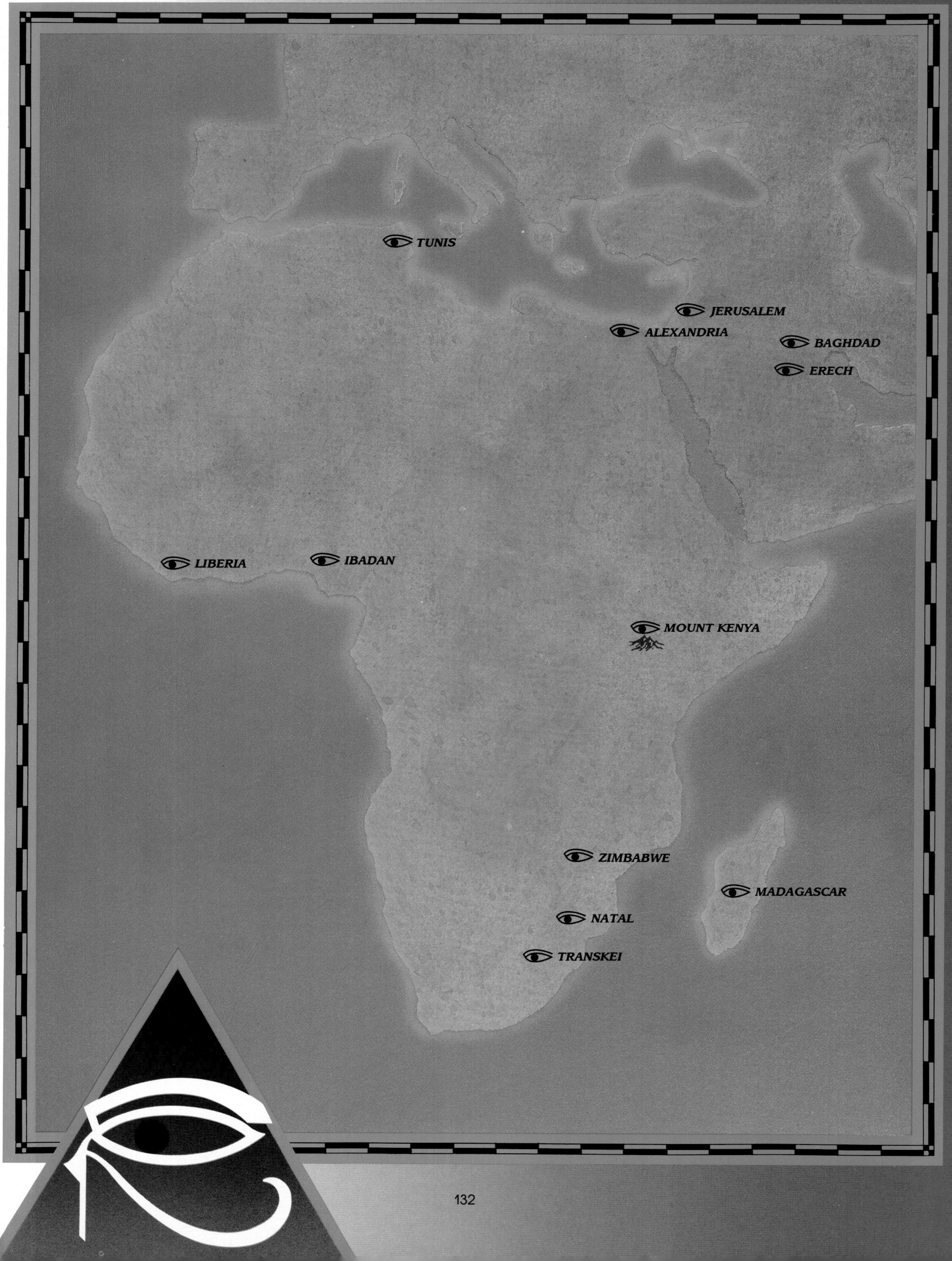

TUNIS

JERUSALEM

ALEXANDRIA

BAGHDAD

ERECH

LIBERIA

IBADAN

MOUNT KENYA

ZIMBABWE

MADAGASCAR

NATAL

TRANSKEI

stitutions, the cult of cargo may have subsided, but it has never disappeared. In 1964 about a third of the 7,000 people of Australian-administered territory of New Hanover began pooling their money to buy American president Lyndon B. Johnson as their new ruler. After little material gain under German, Japanese, and Australian administrations, the islanders reasoned that the leader of the Great Society was far more likely to provide the cargo of their dreams.

The Middle East, long a trading crossroads between Europe, Asia, and Africa, has also been through the ages a crucible of mystical and magical ideas. Alexandria, Egypt, for example, built on the silted expanse of the Nile delta by Alexander the Great, has been a major Mediterranean seaport since the fourth century BC and benefited in its ancient heyday from the confluence of Greek, Egyptian, and Jewish cultures. Those influences made the city an academic capital, with an outstanding university and a great library housing more than 700,000 scrolls. Astrology and alchemy were both reportedly well represented in the library at Alexandria. In the two fields, the melting pot of Alexandria combined disparate traditions into a product that was altogether new.

Relatively few of the secrets of these fledgling occult disciplines have survived, since virtually all the documents were destroyed in a series of Roman invasions. In about AD 290, the Roman emperor Diocletian banned alchemy altogether, apparently out of a fear that it worked all too well. Threatened by unrest in Egypt, he ordered all texts on the subject burned in order to impoverish his reluctant subjects. In the seventh century, those ideas began to coalesce again in the city of Baghdad, the capital of modern-day Iraq. The city lies on the Tigris River about twenty-five miles from the Euphrates. Built on the site of previous cities of the same name, Baghdad was a thriving cultural center almost from its founding in AD 762 as the capital of the Abbasid caliphs. It was also home to scholars who translated and built upon the writings of ancient Greek

Hebrew words in a mystical, sacred Cabalistic Square

Mysticism in Africa and the Middle East

ALEXANDRIA
In the second century, astrologers from the Mediterranean were welcomed in this Egyptian city. Here the renowned astronomer Ptolemy compiled the Tetrabiblos, which became the bible of astrology.

BAGHDAD
Many alchemists worked here in the first years of Islam's expansion, including Abu Musa Jabir ibn Hayyan, known in the West as Geber, whose alchemical experiments advanced knowledge of chemistry.

ERECH
Ruins of ziggurats have been found here and in twenty-nine other ancient cities in present-day Iraq. These towers, built in various shapes, held shrines to the gods; most also served as astrological observatories.

IBADAN
Belief in magic is so strong in this Nigerian town that a company here finds buyers for an item it claims will enable the user to disappear at will.

JERUSALEM
According to Jewish folklore, Solomon's Temple was built here with the help of magical powers that the great king invoked through Cabala, the system of thought by which mystics sought to approach God.

LIBERIA
Benevolent bush spirits are central to this country's village life. Children in "bush schools" learn magic and practical arts such as herbal medicine, farming, and dancing.

MADAGASCAR
Fearing "contagious" magic, in which body parts affect each other even if separated, wealthy persons here once hired servants to ingest their lost blood and nail clippings, to keep enemies from acquiring them.

MOUNT KENYA
Magic reigns in the lands around this peak, home of the Kikuyu. A magic stone used in oath-taking creates obligations so strong and consequences for failing to fulfill them so dire, that oaths are rarely taken.

NATAL
Diviners among the Zulu people of this South African region have a variety of magic potions for treating sick people and animals, about half of them pharmacologically effective.

TRANSKEI
In this region of South Africa, where the Xhosa once destroyed their grain and killed their cattle to regain heavenly favor and rid their lands of Europeans, medicine is mixed with magic and witchcraft.

TUNIS
Sorcerers are popular in this North African capital. They provide potions and talismans, write predictions in the sand, and show believers how to avenge wrongs by sticking pins in wax effigies of enemies.

ZIMBABWE
Exorcism took a turn in the 1950s when this country was a British colony. An African who felt possessed by a European's spirit could be freed only by a complex procedure that included a diet of European food.

philosophers and scientists, particularly in medicine, astronomy, astrology, and alchemy. One of the foremost was Abu Musa Jabir ibn Hayyan, court physician to the caliphs, who became known in the West as Geber.

In the course of his alchemical experimentation, Geber produced a variety of new chemicals, including nitric acid and red oxide of mercury. Elaborating on Aristotle, he taught that all metals were composed of sulfur and mercury, mixed in different proportions—a key idea in later Euro-

pean alchemy. Gold was the perfect combination of these substances. Hence the alchemist's task was to produce chemically pure sulfur and mercury, opening the way to making gold. In later centuries, Arabian lore spread westward in Latin translation, giving rise among other things to much of the European occult tradition.

Far south of the great cities of ancient times, the plains and forests of sub-Saharan Africa harbored their own age-old cultures. Some built permanent structures like the hill

Among the many scholars who gathered at the ancient city of Alexandria, Egypt, pictured below in a fifteenth-century illustration, was the second-century astronomer and astrologer Ptolemy. His astrological writings and elaborate, earth-centered vision of the cosmos (right, in a medieval woodcut) helped lay the foundation for modern astrology.

fortress of Great Zimbabwe. Others lived in scattered villages. Among these were the Bantu-speaking Zulu who lived along the Mfolosi River of what is now Natal province, South Africa, farmers and herders whose living depended on an intimate rapport with the forces of nature.

But these forces were not restricted to weather influences such as rain, wind, or drought. The Zulu forces of nature could also supposedly cause sickness or ill fortune when manipulated by a witch. Such witches were thought to dwell concealed among the Zulu, and it might have seemed to an outsider that the damage from witchcraft was as much in the cure as in the affliction. Once detected, witches were sentenced to immediate death. Their families were likewise exterminated, their crops destroyed, and their cattle confiscated.

Not surprisingly, witches were unlikely to announce themselves. In any event, most were said to be unwittingly inhabited by evil spirits, which might otherwise settle in an animal, a plant, or even a stone. When witchcraft was suspected, the only recourse was to a witch finder, or *isangoma,* a specialist capable of smelling out the parasite.

Because the word of an isangoma was law when it came to identifying witches, the witch finders were feared members of Zulu society. Whenever a Zulu village was visited by disease or bad luck, the chief assembled all the men in a large circle around the isangomas. Daubed with clay and festooned with ornaments, the witch finders danced themselves into a frenzy. Next, all except the chief (who was considered possession proof) joined in a low, continuous chant, so that the isangomas could smell the foul odor of sorcery on the breath of the witches. The witch finders moved around the circle, gnu-tail whips poised to lash out in accusation. When the whips fell, the unfortunate suspect was dragged away, impaled on stakes, and left to die.

According to some accounts, changes in the volume of chanting may have signaled public opinion to the circling isangomas, subtly indicating popular approval of a particular choice—a wealthy but stingy farmer, perhaps, or someone who had broken an important taboo. Others suggest that the isangomas tended to select personal enemies. Whatever the source of the judgment, its validity was apparently acknowledged even by the accused, who are said to have died believing that they had indeed been possessed.

The grisly power of the isangomas was finally broken in the 1820s by Shaka, king of the expanding Zulu nation. During a witch-smelling at Shaka's headquarters at Bulawayo, an isangoma challenged the young ruler's power by singling out two of Shaka's most trusted warriors. That proved to be a fateful error. Not only did the king refuse to turn them over for execution, he also decreed that henceforth no suspected witch could be put to death without royal approval. His subjects need not fear the isangomas, Shaka told them, as long as they proved their loyalty with generous support for his growing army. At a stroke, he had transformed the power of the witches into military strength.

Long after Shaka's death—from assassins in 1828—the army he had saved from the isangomas went on to make modern African history at Isandhlwana, where Zulu warriors wiped out a considerable British force in 1879. Despite that notable outcome, however, African military resistance to the steadily encroaching European settlers was rarely successful. Many Africans, like the Sioux Ghost Dancers on the American plains, believed that only supernatural intervention could save their lands.

Perhaps the most tragic example of that strategy occurred in 1856, when the Xhosa people of what is now South Africa, militarily defeated and further devastated by a cattle lung-disease epidemic, responded eagerly to the news that ghostly visions had been received by a young Xhosa girl named Nonquase.

While scaring birds away from a cornfield, Nonquase reported, she had encountered two men who said they had died long ago. It was their intention to rise from the dead, with other tribal heroes, to drive the whites from the Xhosa land. But first the people must give up witchcraft, then slaughter all their cattle, which had been raised by hands defiled by evil magic. There must be no plowing of the land;

instead, the Xhosa should build stout cattle pens and deep granaries, to hold the bounty that would spring up from the earth. When all these duties had been performed, a great whirlwind would sweep away the unfaithful.

Not all the Xhosa gave full credence to Nonquase's prophecy, their skepticism no doubt bolstered by reluctance to give up their livelihood. Nevertheless, many believers joined in a mass movement, ready to put the good of the Xhosa nation above their individual needs. By some estimates, 400,000 cattle were killed, far more than could be consumed. Dogs and vultures gorged themselves, and everywhere carcasses lay rotting in the sun.

The Xhosa rose early on the date of the prophecy, February 18, 1857, prepared to greet their long-lost friends. Yet the day passed with nothing but disappointment for the gaily bedecked faithful. New dates were set, but the dead did not return, nor were the granaries and cattle pens miraculously filled. Soon the bodies by the wayside were no longer cattle but men, women, and children, dead of starvation.

At least 40,000 Xhosa died in the famine, and by early 1858 another 33,000 had left their lands to seek some means of employment. The now depopulated territory was taken over by the British colonial government, to be parceled out to white settlers.

Regional forms of African magic continued into the twentieth century, when some rituals became a source of renewed pride to black Africans eager to reclaim their own culture. In 1936, twenty-eight years before he became Kenya's first president, a certain Johnstone Kenyatta of the Kikuyu people took a postgraduate anthropology course at the London School of Economics. His professor encouraged Kenyatta to author a book on the Kikuyu people. Kenyatta not only did so, but he changed his missionary-inspired first name to the more Kikuyu-sounding "Jomo."

The result, titled *Facing Mount Kenya,* became popular in Africa and around the world. Honoring and accepting the practices of the Kikuyu—including openly magical rites—the book's highly literate, Western-educated scholar posed proudly on the cover in a Kikuyu monkey-skin robe, holding a spear hastily carved by himself and a friend.

According to Kenyatta's landmark study, the Kikuyu who farmed and hunted on the slopes of Mount Kenya considered magic an everyday affair. In matters as diverse as drought, unrequited love, and healing, Kikuyus often turned for help to the local magician, a respected professional with long years of training.

Most Kikuyu carried a protective charm of some sort, Kenyatta wrote, which was manufactured by a magician. A hunter, for example, might ask for a charm that would pro-

tect him against attack by wild animals. The magician would prepare a mixture of potent herbs, pouring it into a small horn while reciting a special formula. Upon receiving the charm and instructions for using it, the hunter took an oath never to reveal the secrets it entailed. From that time on, he kept the charm on his person; each time he wished to invoke its magic, he passed it over his left shoulder and between his legs seven times, uttering a ritual incantation.

Kikuyu magic provided a variety of means for a lover to win the affection of his or her desired mate, but a man might also seek to use it to become attractive to women in general. According to Kenyatta, a magician asked to weave this powerful spell would demand first that the man vow to the spirits of his ancestors that he would dedicate his life to love: Renouncing all property, he would seek instead to have as many women to love as he could. Whether the elaborate enticement ritual actually worked is a matter of conjecture; less open to question is the fact that a man who resorted to this kind of magic often ended up an outcast in a society that measured a man's success by the way he handled his property and family affairs.

Although the Kikuyu used a wide variety of herbal cures for common ailments, those remedies were considered powerless against certain diseases attributed to an evil spirit of one of the victim's ancestors, which only a magician could locate. By communing with the supreme council of all ancestral spirits, he could drive the tormentor away from the victim, using a combination of magic powders, incantations, and ritual enactments. It was not work that could support a charlatan; payment for a magician's services came only after the sick person got well.

By the time the Kenyans, led by Kenyatta and others, won independence from Britain in 1963, vigorous missionary activity had ensured that much of the nation's population was at least nominally Christian. In many cases, however, the foreign religion coexisted with traditional beliefs, as in a number of resilient folk cultures around the world, from the paper magic of Mexico's Nahua Indians to the mediumistic healing rites of urban Japan. In the last decades of the twentieth century, the practices Kenyatta described in his book remained an accepted part of many Kikuyu lives.

Jomo Kenyatta himself never forgot the apprenticeship he served under his grandfather, a Kikuyu medicine man and former military leader. The realm of magic, Kenyatta wrote in *Facing Mount Kenya,* would always have its place in Kikuyu daily life, for magic enriched ordinary economic and social activities with meaning, connecting them always "to the mysterious forces that surround human life."

Crowned by white clouds, 17,000-foot Mount Kenya (above) towers over the homeland of the Kikuyu people not only physically but spiritually, as the acknowledged home of the great god Ngai. Many Kikuyu magical practices involve Ngai and other gods, who are typically invoked by magicians, or witch doctors, like the one shown here. Wearing a sheepskin hat in this 1980s photograph, the wise man attempts to divine the future by means of a charmed gourd.

ACKNOWLEDGMENTS

The editors wish to thank the following for their assistance: Laura S. Anderberg, Naval Command, Control and Ocean Surveillance Center, San Diego, California; Christophe Barbotin, Conservateur du Département des Antiquités Egyptiennes, Musée du Louvre, Paris, France; Paul Carnahan, Vermont Historical Society, Montpelier, Vermont; Ferdinand Freiherr von Lamezan, Hamburg, Germany; Ingeborg Hermeling, Bad Meinberg, Germany; Bernard Heuvelmans, Centre de Cryptozoologie, Le Vesinet, France; Gérard Leser, Université Populaire du Rhin, Mulhouse, France; Roy P. Mackal, Chicago, Illinois; Robert W. Morgan, Whitefish, Montana; Ulla Oscarsson, Curator Jämtlands Läns Museum, Östersund, Sweden; Volker Schuhmacher, Institut für Grenzgebiete der Psychologie und Psychohygiene, Freiburg, Germany.

PICTURE CREDITS

BIBLIOGRAPHY

Alexander, John, Ghosts: Washington's Most Famous Ghost Stories. Arlington, Va.: Washington Book Trading, 1988.
America's Fascinating Indian Heritage. Pleasantville, N.Y.: Reader's Digest, 1978.
Archer, Jules, African Firebrand. New York: Julian Messner, 1969.
Ashe, Geoffrey:
    Camelot and the Vision of Albion. New York: St. Martin's Press, 1971.
    Do What You Will. London: W. H. Allen, 1974.
Baker, Margaret, Folklore of the Sea. North Pomfret, Vt.: David & Charles, 1979.
Barker, Godfrey, "Fraser Trust's £1½ m. Buys Iona for Nation." Daily Telegraph, May 25, 1979.
Barrett, Charles, The Bunyip and Other Mythical Monsters and Legends. Melbourne: Reed and Harris, 1946.
Bean, George Ewart, Aegean Turkey. New York: W. W. Norton, 1979.
" 'Beast of Truro' Mystifying Cape Cod." New York Times, January 17, 1982.
Berlitz, Charles:
    The Bermuda Triangle. Garden City, N.Y.: Doubleday, 1974.
    The Dragon's Triangle. New York: Wynwood Press, 1989.

Berry, Steve, "Ancient Site Wins Heritage Designation." *Vancouver Province,* October 2, 1991.

"The Black Hills, Once Hunting Grounds of the Red Men." *National Geographic,* September 1927.

Bord, Janet, and Colin Bord, *Alien Animals.* Harrisburg, Pa.: Stackpole Books, 1981.

Bosi, Roberto, *The Lapps.* New York: Frederick A. Praeger, 1960.

Boucher, Alan, transl., *Ghosts, Witchcraft and the Other World.* Reykjavik, Iceland: *Iceland Review,* 1977.

Bray, Warwick, *Everyday Life of the Aztecs.* New York: Dorset Press, 1987.

Bray, Warwick, Earl H. Swanson, and Ian S. Farrington, *The New World.* New York: E. P. Dutton, 1975.

Bringsvaerd, Tor Åge, *Phantoms and Fairies.* Oslo: Tanum-Norli, 1979.

Brooks, Lester, *Great Civilizations of Ancient Africa.* New York: Four Winds Press, 1972.

Brun, Viggo and Trond Schumacher, *Traditional Herbal Medicine in Northern Thailand.* Berkeley, Calif.: University of California, 1987.

Burman, Jose, *Disaster Struck South Africa.* Cape Town: C. Struik, 1971.

Cameron, Ian, *Kingdom of the Sun God.* New York: Facts on File, 1990.

Casson, Lionel, *Ancient Egypt* (Great Ages of Man series). New York: Time, 1965.

Cavendish, Richard, ed., *Man, Myth & Magic.* New York: Marshall Cavendish, 1985.

Chamberlain, Basil Hall, *Japanese Things.* Rutland, Vt.: Charles E. Tuttle, 1904.

Childress, David Hatcher, *Lost Cities and Ancient Mysteries of South America.* Stelle, Ill.: Adventures Unlimited Press, no date.

Christiansen, Palle, *The Melanesian Cargo Cult: Millenarianism as a Factor in Cultural Change.* Transl. by John R. B. Gosney. Copenhagen: Akademisk Forlag, 1969.

Clanton-Collins, Jan, "An Interview with Burnam Burnam." *Shaman's Drum,* Mid-Fall 1988.

Cohen, Daniel:
The Encyclopedia of Ghosts. New York: Dodd, Mead, 1981.
The Encyclopedia of Monsters. New York: Dodd, Mead, 1982.
The Encyclopedia of the Strange. New York: Dodd, Mead, 1985.

Coleman, Loren, "The Menehune." *Fate,* July 1989.

Collinder, Björn, *The Lapps.* Princeton, N.J.: Princeton University Press, 1949.

Cook, Elizabeth, "Politics and the Oral Traditions of the Tribes." *Wicazo-Sa Review,* 1987.

Cosmic Connections (Mysteries of the Unknown series). Alexandria, Va.: Time-Life Books, 1988.

Costello, Peter, *In Search of Lake Monsters.* London: Garnstone Press, 1974.

Crowl, Philip A., *The Intelligent Traveller's Guide to Historic Scotland.* New York: Congdon & Weed, 1986.

Davidson, Basil, *The African Genius.* Boston: Little, Brown, 1969.

Davidson, Basil, and the Editors of Time-Life Books, *African Kingdoms.* New York: Time, 1966.

Davis, Winston, *Dojo.* Stanford, Calif.: Stanford University Press, 1980.

Dethier, Michel, and Ayako Dethier-Sakamoto, "The Tzuchinoko, an Unidentified Snake from Japan." International Society of Cryptozoology, 1987.

Downer, Craig C., "The Horrible Ghost of Anchicaya." *Fate,* March 1982.

Dunsford, John, "£600,000 Offered for Island 'Cradle of Christianity.'" *Daily Telegraph,* April 23, 1979.

Du Plessis, I. D., *Poltergeists of the South.* Cape Town: Howard Timmins, 1966.

Earth Energies (Mysteries of the Unknown series). Alexandria, Va.: Time-Life Books, 1991.

Eberhart, George M., *Monsters.* New York: Garland, 1983.

Eliade, Mircea, *Shamanism.* Transl. by Willard R. Trask. Princeton, N.J.: Princeton University Press, 1964.

Eliade, Mircea, ed., *The Encyclopedia of Religion.* New York: Macmillan, 1987.

El Mahdy, Christine, *Mummies, Myth and Magic in Ancient Egypt.* New York: Thames and Hudson, 1989.

Encyclopaedia Britannica. Chicago: William Benton, 1961.

Erman, Adolf, *Life in Ancient Egypt.* New York: Dover, 1971.

Fabricius, Johannes, *Alchemy.* Wellingborough, Northamptonshire, England: Aquarian, 1976.

Fagan, Brian, *Elusive Treasure.* New York: Charles Scribner's Sons, 1977.

Farquhar, Michael, "The Haunt of Fort McNair." *Washington Post,* October 31, 1991.

Feats and Wisdom of the Ancients (Library of Curious and Unusual Facts series). Alexandria, Va.: Time-Life Books, 1990.

Finlay, Ian, *The Highlands.* London: B. T. Batsford, 1963.

Folklore, Myths and Legends of Britain. London: Reader's Digest, 1973.

Fontenrose, Joseph, *The Delphic Oracle.* Berkeley: University of California, 1978.

Forman, Joan, *Haunted Royal Homes.* London: Harrap, 1987.

Forman, Sheila, *Scottish Country Houses & Castles.* Glasgow: Collins, 1971.

Fraser, George MacDonald, *Flashman and the Mountain of Light.* New York: Alfred A. Knopf, 1991.

Frye, Richard N., *The Heritage of Persia.* London: Readers Union, Weidenfeld and Nicolson, 1962.

Fulcanelli, *Le Mystère des Cathédrales.* Transl. by Mary Sworder. Albuquerque, N.Mex.: Brotherhood of Life, 1984.

Gerster, Georg, "Searching Out Medieval Churches in Ethiopia's Wilds." *National Geographic,* December 1970.

"Giant Octopus Blamed for Deep Sea Fishing Disruptions." *International Society of Cryptozoology Newsletter,* Autumn 1985.

Golomb, Louis, *An Anthropology of Curing in Multiethnic Thailand.* Illinois Studies in Anthropology, No. 15, 1985.

González-Wippler, Migene, *Santería: The Religion.* New York: Harmony, 1989.

Gordon, Anne Wolrige, *Dame Flora.* London: Hodder and Stoughton, 1974.

Gordon, David G., "What Is That?" *Oceans,* July-August 1987.

Grant, I. F., *The Macleods.* London: Faber & Faber, 1959.

Grant, Michael, *A Guide to the Ancient World.* New York: H. W. Wilson, 1986.

Gray, Affleck, *The Big Grey Man of Ben Macdhui.* Aberdeen: Impulse Books, 1970.

Green, John, *Sasquatch.* Seattle: Hancock House, 1978.

Greenfield, R. H., "Iona Goes up for Public Sale—Morman Bid of £2m Reported." *Southern Telegraph,* April 15, 1979.

Griswold, A. B., "The Rishis of Wat Pó." *Felicitation Volumes of Southeast Asian Studies Presented to His Highness Prince Dhaninivat on the Occasion of His Eighteenth Birthday* (Vol. 1). Bangkok: The Siam Society, 1965.

Group, David, *The Evidence for the Bermuda Triangle.* Wellingborough, Northamptonshire, England: Aquarian Press, 1984.

Haining, Peter, *A Dictionary of Ghosts.* London: Robert Hale, 1982.

Harlan, Harry V., "A Caravan Journey through Abyssinia." *National Geographic,* June 1925.

Harner, Michael J., *The Jívaro.* Garden City, N.Y.: Doubleday/Natural History Press, 1972.

Harpur, James, and Jennifer Westwood, *The Atlas of Legendary Places.* New York: Weidenfeld and Nicolson, 1989.

Hassrick, Royal B., *The Sioux.* Norman: University of Oklahoma Press, 1964.

Helm, Mike, *Oregon's Ghosts & Monsters.* Eugene, Ore.: Rainy Day Press, 1983.

Hennigar, "Ted" R., *Scotian Spooks, Mystery and Violence.* Hantsport, Nova Scotia, 1978.

Herald, Albany, *The Highland Clans.* Rugby, England: Bramhall House, 1977.

Heuvelmans, Bernard:
Annotated Checklist of Apparently Unknown Animals with Which Cryptozoology Is Concerned. Le Bugue, France: International Society of Cryptozoology, 1986.
In the Wake of the Sea-Serpents. Transl. by Richard Garnett. New York: Hill and Wang, 1965.
On the Track of Unknown Animals. New York: Hill and Wang, 1958.

Hillerman, Tony, "Sacred Ground." *National Geographic Traveler,* May-June 1989.

Hori, Ichiro, *Folk Religion in Japan.* Tokyo: University of Tokyo Press, 1968.

Hudson, Rex A., and Dennis M. Hanratty, eds., *Bolivia: A Country Study.* Washington, D.C.: Federal Research Division, Library of Congress, 1989.

Hunter, C. Bruce, *A Guide to Ancient Mexican Ruins.* Norman: University of Oklahoma Press, 1977.

Huot, Jean-Louis, *Persia* (Vol. 1). Transl. by H. S. B. Harrison. Geneva: Nagel, 1965.

"Island for Sale." *Time,* March 19, 1979.

Johnson, Kenneth Rayner, *The Fulcanelli Phenomenon.* Jersey, Channel Islands: Neville Spearman, 1980.

Jones, Louis V., *The Clubs of the Georgian Rakes.* New York: Columbia University Press, 1942.

Kenyatta, Jomo, *Facing Mount Kenya.* New York: Vintage Books, 1965.

La Barre, Weston, *The Ghost Dance.* Garden City, N.Y.: Doubleday, 1970.

Lavender, David, *The Great West.* New York: American Heritage, 1965.

Leake, Christopher, "Death Duty Brings U.S. Bid for Scottish Isle." *Daily Telegraph,* March 10, 1979.

Leonard, Jonathan Norton, *Ancient America* (Great Ages of Man series). New York: Time, 1967.

Lhote, Henri, *The Search for the Tassili Frescoes.* Transl. by Alan Houghton Brodrick. New York: E. P. Dutton, 1959.

Luomala, Katharine, *The Menehune of Polynesia and Other Mythical Little People of Oceania.* Honolulu: Bernice P. Bishop Museum, 1951.

McEwan, Graham J., *Mystery Animals of Britain and Ireland.* London: Robert Hale, 1986.

MacGregor, Rob, and Trish Janeshutz, "Abducted by a Ghost Ship." *Fate,* May 1984.

McIntyre, Loren, "The Lost Empire of the Incas." *National Geographic,* December 1973.

Mackal, Roy P., *Searching for Hidden Animals.* Garden City, N.Y.: Doubleday, 1980.

Macnaghten, Angus, *Haunted Berkshire.* Newbury, Berkshire: Countryside Books, 1986.

Markotic, Vladimir, and Grover Krantz, eds., *The Sasquatch and Other Unknown Hominoids.* Calgary, Alberta, Canada: Western Publishers, 1984.

Marsden, Simon, *The Haunted Realm.* New York: E. P. Dutton, 1986.

Martyr, Deborah, "An Investigation of the Orang-Pendek, the 'Short Man' of Sumatra." *Cryptozoology,* No. 9, 1990.

Mason, Herbert Molloy, Jr., *Secrets of the Supernatural.* New York: Four Winds Press, 1975.

Matheson, Sylvia A., *Persia, An Archaeological Guide.* London: Faber and Faber, 1979.

Matthews, John, *The Grail.* New York: Crossroad, 1981.

Maxwell, James A., ed., *America's Fascinating Indian Heritage.* Pleasantville, N.Y.: Reader's Digest, 1978.

Mead, Charles W., *Old Civilizations of Inca Land.* New York: Cooper Square, 1972.

Meurger, Michel, "In Jormungandra's Coils: A Cultural Archaeology of the Norse Sea-Serpent." *Fortean Times,* Winter 1988-1989.

Michell, John, *The Earth Spirit.* New York: Crossroad, 1978.

"Miraculous Perception." *Time,* August 5, 1991.

Morris, Donald R., *The Washing of the Spears.* New York: Simon & Schuster, 1965.

Morshead, Sir Owen, *Windsor Castle.* London: Phaidon Press, 1951.

Mullikin, Mary Augusta, "Tai Shan, Sacred Mountain of the East." *National Geographic,* June 1945.

Murphy, Joseph M., *Santería.* Boston: Beacon Press, 1988.

Myers, Arthur, *The Ghostly Register.* Chicago: Contemporary Books, 1986.

The New Encyclopaedia Britannica (Vol. 6). Chicago: Encyclopaedia Britannica, 1984.

Norman, Diana, *Tom Corbett's Stately Ghosts of England.* New York: Taplinger, 1970.

Poole, Keith B.:
Britain's Haunted Heritage. London: Robert Hale, 1988.
Ghosts of Wessex. London: David & Charles, 1976.
Sunday Express, July 26, 1970.

Powell, Neil, *Alchemy, the Ancient Science.* Garden City, N.Y.: Doubleday, 1976.

Pugh, Jane, *Welsh Ghosts, Poltergeists and Demons.* Jane Pugh, 1978.

Quest for the Past. Pleasantville, N.Y.: Reader's Digest, 1984.

Ritter, E. A., *Shaka Zulu.* Middlesex, England: Penguin,

1987.

Rogers, Tom, "The Black Hills: Where the Buffalo Roam." *National Geographic Traveler,* Spring 1985.

Rowland, Bob:
"Answers to Apparition Elusive." *San Diego Union,* July 24, 1991.
"Darkened Billboard Still Lures Crowd to Chula Vista." *Los Angeles Times,* July 23, 1991.

St. Clair, Sheila, "A Noisy Night in Ireland." *Fate,* February 1984.

Sanderson, Ivan T., *Abominable Snowmen: Legend Come to Life.* Philadelphia: Chilton, 1961.

Sandstrom, Alan R., and Pamela Effrein Sandstrom, *Traditional Papermaking and Paper Cult Figures of Mexico.* Norman: University of Oklahoma Press, 1986.

Scholefield, Alan, *The Dark Kingdoms.* New York: William Morrow, 1975.

Schultheis, Rob, *The Hidden West: Journeys in the American Outback.* New York: Random House, 1982.

Secrets of the Alchemists (Mysteries of the Unknown series). Alexandria, Va.: Time-Life Books, 1990.

Service, Alastair, and Jean Bradbery, *A Guide to the Megaliths of Europe.* London: Granada, 1979.

Sherwood, Roland H., *Maritime Mysteries.* Windsor, Nova Scotia: Lancelot Press, 1976.

Soustelle, Jacques, *Daily Life of the Aztecs.* Transl. by Patrick O'Brian. Stanford, Calif.: Stanford University Press, 1961.

The SS (The Third Reich series). Alexandria, Va.: Time-Life Books, 1988.

Steiner, Robert, "A Canadian Town Is Less Monolithic Thanks to a Big Rock." *Wall Street Journal,* October 30, 1991.

Stevenson, John, *Yoshitoshi's Thirty-Six Ghosts.* New York: Weatherhill/Blue Tiger, 1983.

Stoneham, C. T., *Wanderings in Wild Africa.* London: Hutchinson & Company, 1932.

Strange Stories and Amazing Facts. Pleasantville, N.Y.: Reader's Digest, 1984.

Strelan, John G., *Search for Salvation.* Adelaide, Australia: Lutheran, 1977.

Stuart, George E., and Gene S. Stuart, *Discovering Man's Past in the Americas.* Washington, D.C.: National Geographic, 1969.

Swan, James A., *The Power of Place.* Wheaton, Ill.: Quest Books, 1991.

Taylor, Leighton R., "Megamouth—A New Species, Genus, and Family of Lamnoid Shark from the Hawaiian Islands." *Proceedings of the California Academy of Sciences,* July 6, 1983.

Thompson, Leonard, *A History of South Africa.* New Haven, Conn.: Yale University Press, 1990.

Tierney, Patrick, *The Highest Altar.* London: Bloomsbury, 1989.

Time and Space (Mysteries of the Unknown series). Alexandria, Va.: Time-Life Books, 1990.

Towers, Eric, *Dashwood: The Man and the Myth.* Wellingborough, Northamptonshire, England: Aquarian Press, 1986.

Underwood, Peter, *A Gazetteer of British, Scottish and Irish Ghosts.* New York: Bell, 1973.

Van Zandt, Eleanor, and Roy Stemman, *Mysteries of the Lost Lands.* London: Aldus, 1976.

Viola, Herman J., *After Columbus.* Washington, D.C.: Smithsonian Books, 1990.

Visions and Prophecies (Mysteries of the Unknown series). Alexandria, Va.: Time-Life Books, 1988.

Waldie, Paula, " 'Breathing Room' for Indian-Site Park Lobby." *Vancouver Province,* July 21, 1991.

Webster's New Biographical Dictionary. Springfield, Mass.: Merriam-Webster, 1988.

Weir, Tom, *The Western Highlands.* London: B. T. Batsford, 1973.

Welfare, Simon, and John Fairley, *Arthur C. Clarke's Mysterious World.* New York: A & W, 1980.

Wepman, Dennis, *Jomo Kenyatta.* New York: Chelsea House, 1985.

Wernick, Robert, *The Monument Builders* (The Emergence of Man series). New York: Time-Life Books, 1973.

Westwood, Jennifer, ed., *The Atlas of Mysterious Places.* New York: Weidenfeld & Nicolson, 1987.

Whitaker, Terence, *Haunted England.* Chicago: Contemporary Books, 1987.

Wilkinson, Philip, *The Time-Life Encyclopedia of Mysterious Places.* Alexandria, Va.: Time-Life Books, 1990.

Wilson, Colin, *Enigmas and Mysteries.* Garden City, N.Y.: Doubleday, 1976.

Worsley, Peter, *The Trumpet Shall Sound.* New York: Schocken, 1968.

Zarzynski, Joseph W., *Champ—Beyond the Legend.* Port Henry, N.Y.: Bannister, 1984.

INDEX

Time-Life Books is a division of Time Life Inc.,
a wholly owned subsidiary of
THE TIME INC. BOOK COMPANY

TIME-LIFE BOOKS

PRESIDENT: Mary N. Davis

MANAGING EDITOR: Thomas H. Flaherty
Director of Editorial Resources: Elise D. Ritter-Clough
Executive Art Director: Ellen Robling
Director of Photography and Research: John Conrad Weiser
Editorial Board: Dale M. Brown, Janet Cave, Roberta Conlan, Laura Foreman, Jim Hicks, Blaine Marshall, Rita Thievon Mullin, Henry Woodhead
Assistant Director of Editorial Resources/Training Manager: Norma E. Shaw

PUBLISHER: Robert H. Smith

Associate Publisher: Sandra Lafe Smith
Editorial Director: Russell B. Adams, Jr.
Marketing Director: Anne C. Everhart
Director of Production Services: Robert N. Carr
Production Manager: Prudence G. Harris
Supervisor of Quality Control: James King

Editorial Operations
Production: Celia Beattie
Library: Louise D. Forstall
Computer Composition: Deborah G. Tait (Manager), Monika D. Thayer, Janet Barnes Syring, Lillian Daniels
Interactive Media Specialist: Patti H. Cass

Library of Congress Cataloging in Publication Data
The Mysterious world / by the editors of Time-Life Books.
    p. cm. — (Mysteries of the unknown)
Includes bibliographical references.
ISBN 0-8094-6549-3 (trade)
ISBN 0-8094-6550-7 (library)
1. Parapsychology and geography.
2. Sacred space.   3. Monsters.   4. Ghosts.
I. Time-Life Books.   II. Series.
BF1045.G46M97 1992
133—dc20   92-20196
                                               CIP

MYSTERIES OF THE UNKNOWN

SERIES EDITOR: Jim Hicks
Series Administrators: Barbara Levitt, Judith W. Shanks
Senior Art Director: Thomas S. Huestis
Picture Editor: Paula York-Soderlund

Editorial Staff for *The Mysterious World*
Text Editors: Esther Ferington (principal), Paul Mathless
Associate Editors/Research: Christian D. Kinney, Dan Kulpinski
Assistant Art Director: Lorraine D. Rivard
Writers: Charles J. Hagner, Sarah D. Ince
Copy Coordinators: Donna Carey, Juli Duncan
Picture Coordinators: David A. Herod, Greg S. Johnson
Editorial Assistant: Julia Kendrick

Special Contributors: Tom DiGiovanni, Ann Louise Gates, Richard Greenwell, Patricia A. Paterno, Evelyn S. Prettyman, Nancy J. Seeger (research); Roberta Conlan, Donal Kevin Gordon, Harvey Loomis, Susan Perry, Peter Pocock (text); John Drummond (design); Hazel Blumberg-McKee (index).

Correspondents: Elisabeth Kraemer-Singh (Bonn), Christine Hinze (London), Christina Lieberman (New York), Maria Vincenza Aloisi (Paris), Ann Natanson (Rome).
Valuable assistance was also provided by Angelika Lemmer (Bonn); Nihal Tamraz (Cairo); Bing Wong (Hong Kong); Judy Aspinall (London); Trini Bandres (Madrid); Juan Sosa (Moscow); Elizabeth Brown, Katheryn White (New York); Dag Christensen (Oslo); John Maier (Rio de Janeiro); Ann Wise, Leonora Dodsworth (Rome); Mary Johnson (Stockholm); Dick Berry (Tokyo); Traudl Lessing (Vienna).

Other Publications:

For information on and a full description of any of the Time-Life Books series listed above, please call 1-800-621-7026 or write:
Reader Information
Time-Life Customer Service
P.O. Box C-32068
Richmond, Virginia 23261-2068

This volume is one of a series that examines the history and nature of seemingly paranormal phenomena. Other books in the series include: